NET-CENTRIC APPROACHES TO INTELLIGENCE AND NATIONAL SECURITY

NET-CENTRIC APPROACHES TO INTELLIGENCE AND NATIONAL SECURITY

edited by

Roy Ladner
Naval Research Laboratory
Stennis Space Center

Frederick E. Petry
Naval Research Laboratory
Stennis Space Center
and
Tulane University

 Springer

Roy Ladner
Naval Research Laboratory
Stennis Space Center, MS 39529

Frederick E. Petry
Naval Research Laboratory
Stennis Space Center, MS 39529

Library of Congress Cataloging-in-Publication Data

A C.I.P. Catalogue record for this book is available
from the Library of Congress.

Net-Centric Approaches to Intelligence and National Security
edited by Roy Ladner and Frederick E. Petry

ISBN-10: 0-387-24295-3   e-ISBN-10: 0-387-26176-1
ISBN-13: 978-0-387-24295-8   e-ISBN-13: 978-0-387-26176-8

Printed on acid-free paper.

Printed in the United States of America.

9 8 7 6 5 4 3 2 1   SPIN 11374800, 11495048

springeronline.com

To

  Jane

    - Roy Ladner

To

  Dottie, John and Christine

    - Fred Petry

TABLE OF CONTENTS

Preface

The development of net-centric approaches for intelligence and national security applications has become a major concern in many areas such as defense, intelligence and national and international law enforcement agencies. In this volume we consider the web architectures and recent developments that make net-centric approaches for intelligence and national security possible. These include developments in information integration and recent advances in web services including the concept of the semantic web. Discovery, analysis and management of web-available data pose a number of interesting challenges for research in web-based management systems. Intelligent agents and data mining are some of the techniques that can be employed. A number of specific systems that are net-centric based in various areas of military applications, intelligence and law enforcement are presented that utilize one or more of such techniques

The opening chapter overviews the concepts related to ontologies which now form much of the basis of the possibility of sharing of information in the Semantic Web. In the next chapter an overview of Web Services and examples of the use of Web Services for net-centric operations as applied to meteorological and oceanographic (MetOc) data is presented and issues related to the Navy's use of MetOc Web Services are discussed. The third chapter focuses on metadata as conceived to support the concepts of a service-oriented architecture and, in particular, as it relates to the DoD Net-Centric Data Strategy and the NCES core services. The potential benefits for homeland security applications from integrated and interoperable geographic data sources. are described in chapter 4 This is then illustrated by a description of the Naval Research Laboratory's Geospatial Information Database (GIDB®). The following chapter discusses next generation net-centric information sharing and analytical systems that are being created and deployed to better address issues of terrorism, money laundering, narcotics trafficking, and fraud investigations utilizing visualization approaches. Next, chapter 6 describes the current state-of-the-art in web services technology and its role in the Global Information Grid (GIG). It also discusses a GIG prototype supporting web-service enabled interoperability between a military system, simulation and intelligent agents for Course of Action Analysis. On both the public Internet and private Intranets, there is a vast amount of data available that is owned and maintained by different organizations, distributed all around the world. These data resources are rich and recent; however, information gathering and knowledge discovery from them, in a particular knowledge domain, confronts major difficulties. The objective of chapter 7 is to introduce an intelligent agent approach to provide for domain-specific information gathering and integration from multiple distributed sources. Finally chapter 8 describes current and future solutions to providing representations of the natural environment in modeling and simulation architectures for DoD applications in the semantic web context. An ontology of physics is discussed in order to provide a more abstract semantic description scheme for representing both models of the natural environment and their data.

We wish to thank all of our chapter contributors for their excellent submissions and their patience with the final production process.

Roy Ladner
Fred Petry

Chapter 1

ONTOLOGIES FOR THE SEMANTIC WEB

Vipin S. Menon[1], Roy Ladner[2] and Frederick E. Petry[2]
[1]Electrical Engineering and Computer Science Department
Tulane University, New Orleans, LA 70118

[2]U.S. Naval Research Laboratory,
Stennis Space Center, MS 39529

Abstract: Over approximately the last decade, the extraordinary and explosive growth of
             the Internet has dramatically altered our perception of computing. The amount
             of information available at the click of a mouse button is immense, and
             oftentimes unmanageable. There is a requirement for approaches to bring
             order to chaos, to organize information so that it provides value and meaning,
             and to answer questions hitherto considered impossible to answer. This is
             precisely where ontologies play a role. Ontologies restore order to chaotic
             collections of data by neatly and systematically arranging and classifying data
             into meaningful hierarchies, and by enabling the merging of dissimilar and
             seemingly disparate sources of information, thus producing answers to
             complex queries.

Key words: Ontologies, Concept Hierarchy, Information Integration, Interoperability,
             Vocabulary, Synonyms, Thesaurus, HTML, XML, RDF, OWL, Semantic
             Web, W3C

1.   INTRODUCTION

A key aspect to the net-centric future for intelligence and security applications is a capability to share and access data from the ever-expanding multitude of sites available on the semantic web. The very nature of the web dictates that to continue its evolution by growth of the number of web sites, centralized control is neither feasible nor desirable, but mutual interoperability is. Interoperability among such sites is being facilitated by the development of ontologies that can express data semantics in languages such as OWL. In this chapter we will give a broad view of the concepts related to ontologies to provide an introduction for various applications described in the following chapters.

The word 'ontology' originated in philosophy and is used to mean a theory of the nature of existence or the science of being. In particular, it describes what types of things can exist. The artificial intelligence research community has adapted the word to mean the following:

- An ontology is a *formal shared conceptualization* of a particular domain of interest. [1]

- An ontology is an explicit *specification of an abstract, simplified view of a world we desire to represent.* [2]

So the term ontology often has been used to refer to the application of artificial intelligence techniques to databases for performing data mining, data integration, data merging, in order to produce meaningful analyses and enrich the meaning of already existing data. It is this latter sense of the utilization of ontologies as metadata for various data sources on the semantic web [3] that has become an area of extreme current interest and the focus of the topics of this volume.

2.   WHAT IS AN ONTOLOGY?

It is hard to present all the properties of an ontology in a simple listing. Therefore, in this section we first need to discuss the general nature of ontologies and understand how an ontology can be viewed as a hierarchy. Finally we examine the components of an ontology, with the help of a simple yet concrete example ontology.

2.1   The Nature of Ontologies

Ontologies are inherently subjective. In this respect, ontologies are similar to the observations made by human beings. Two persons observing the same universe around them may form two completely different views of the proceedings around them. Similarly, two ontologies O_1 and O_2 may be quite different, even though both of them are inherently representing the same underlying data. It might even be difficult to say which of O_1 or O_2 is better. This relative usefulness would depend on the particular application for which the ontology is used. In addition, it might even depend on the particular individual who is using the ontology at a certain point in time.

An ideal ontological system is difficult to specify exactly and is a concept that exists only in the mind of some researchers. A perfect ontological system (one that could handle any kinds of queries about any kinds of objects from any user), would require a much deeper understanding of knowledge conceptualization and natural language processing than research directions can support in the feasible future. The fact that ontologies are such an active area of research with immense potential, illustrates, among other things, that the generation of good ontologies is certainly non-trivial.

Building ontologies is typically difficult, time-consuming and expensive. This is especially so, if the goal is to construct an ontology that is rich and powerful enough to perform automated inferencing. Construction of such an ontology requires careful attention to detail and a strong ability to organize information meaningfully.

Since an ontology organizes things into a clean and well-defined hierarchy, hidden, implicit and unknown design criteria are often uncovered, thus promoting an openness. This is facilitated by an ontology's use of common terms, meanings and an agreed upon vocabulary, to make it's concepts more explicit.

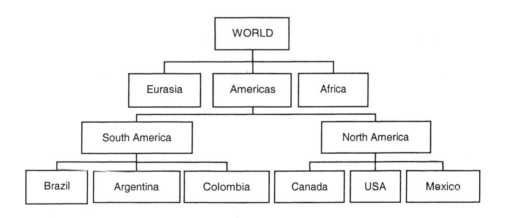

Figure 1-1. A Simple Concept Hierarchy Showing Continents and Countries

Organizing concepts into a hierarchy is a key aspect of building ontologies. The idea is similar to the processes of abstraction and inheritance in object-oriented programming. Ontology development often follows a bottom-up strategy where we may specify properties by first identifying instances, and then using these instances to extract meaningful general properties.   Thus we glean all the little details, and extract a big picture from it.

2.2   The Components of an Ontology

Ontologies are typically useful when interactions occur such as the ones listed below

i) between human beings,

ii) between computers containing intelligent agents,

iii) between humans and intelligent agents.

In order to facilitate such interactions, an ontology   must have the following components: _
             a vocabulary, a dictionary and a set of rules (axioms).
Then they must be a represented in a form that can be unambiguously interpreted and processed by a computer.

So we can see that ontologies foster shared understanding.. By using an agreed-upon vocabulary, ontologies provide the vocabulary needed for negotiation. Usage of the same terms, meanings and rules facilitates a shared understanding of the domain of interest.

The three key components of an ontology are illustrated in Figure 2 where we see:

1) A dictionary : A list of terms (vocabulary) that need to be defined clearly, along with their agreed-upon meanings

2) A set of lexical entries – labels, synonyms, stems, textual documentation, etc.

Two terms having the same meanings are known as *synonyms*. An ontology typically has a thesauru*s*, where words and their corresponding synonyms are stored.   Two terms having opposite meanings are known as *antonyms*. e.g. good, bad.   Two terms that sound similar, but having different meanings, and are possibly spelled differently are known as *homonyms*. e.g. vice, vise

3) A set of rules for drawing inferences, and possibly to be used in the merging of ontologies.

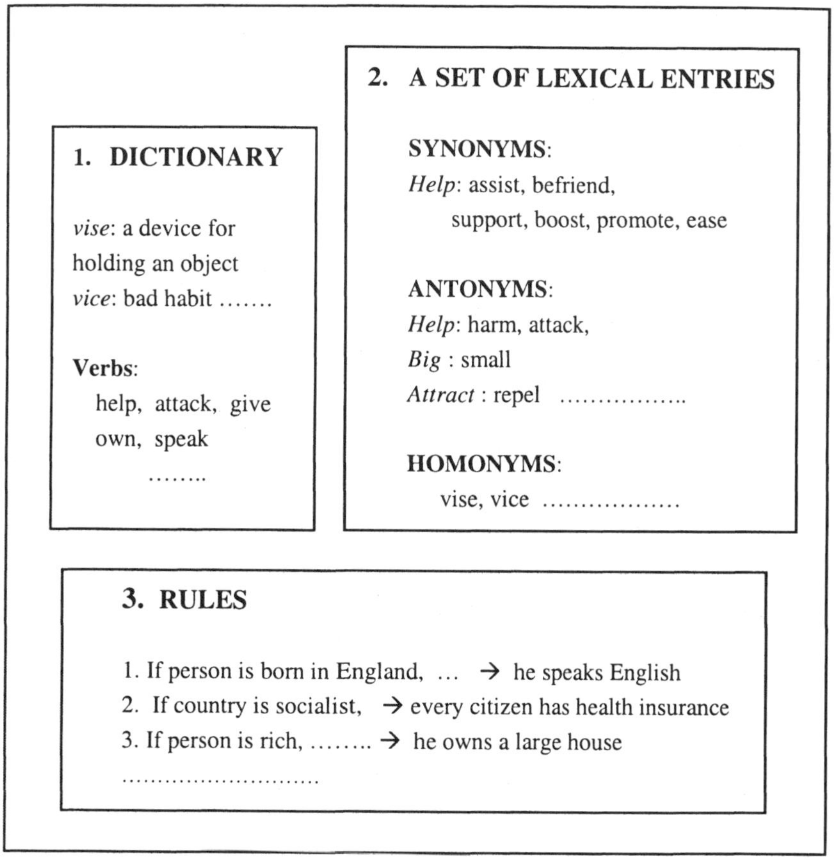

```
+-----------------------------------------------------------------------+
|                                                                       |
|                         +-------------------------------------------+ |
|                         |  2.  A SET OF LEXICAL ENTRIES             | |
|  +-------------------+   |                                          | |
|  |  1.  DICTIONARY   |   |  SYNONYMS:                               | |
|  |                   |   |  Help: assist, befriend,                 | |
|  |  vise: a device   |   |         support, boost, promote, ease    | |
|  |  for holding an   |   |                                          | |
|  |  object           |   |  ANTONYMS:                               | |
|  |  vice: bad habit  |   |  Help: harm, attack,                     | |
|  |  .......          |   |  Big : small                             | |
|  |                   |   |  Attract : repel  ................       | |
|  |  Verbs:           |   |                                          | |
|  |    help, attack,  |   |  HOMONYMS:                               | |
|  |    give own, speak|   |       vise, vice  ................       | |
|  |       ........    |   |                                          | |
|  +-------------------+   +------------------------------------------+ |
|                                                                       |
|   +-----------------------------------------------------------------+ |
|   |   3.  RULES                                                     | |
|   |                                                                | |
|   |   1. If person is born in England,  ...  → he speaks English   | |
|   |   2. If country is socialist,  → every citizen has health      | |
|   |      insurance                                                 | |
|   |   3. If person is rich, ........ → he owns a large house        | |
|   |      ..........................                                | |
|   +-----------------------------------------------------------------+ |
+-----------------------------------------------------------------------+
```

Figure 1-2. A Snapshot of Segments of a Simple Ontology

3.   APPLICATIONS OF ONTOLGIES

In this section we see how ontologies apply to various problems for which they have developed. The issues that arise in the merging or integration of ontologies are first presented. Then a consideration of the utilization of ontologies as a classification system is described. Finally their usage in our main interest here, the semantic web is overviewed.

3.1   Ontology Merging Issues

Anticipation of the possibility of collaborations is a major motivation for the development of an ontology. An ontology is typically created for a specific domain of interest. Depending on the area, this domain may be very narrow or limited in scope. It is not expected that a single ontology could apply to wide range of problems. Implicitly, this means that for larger tasks (tasks that involve wider vision) we would need to use data from different ontologies. In other words, an assumption is made that different ontologies would have to collaborate (perhaps by being merged) to produce meaningful information.

Information integration is a key goal of ontologies. Ontologies can be used to integrate information from heterogeneous sources and databases such as in data warehouses and federated databases. Both structural heterogeneity (differences in the structure of data) and semantic heterogeneity (differences in meanings assigned to the same valid syntactic name) could be overcome with the use of an appropriate ontology.

In order to be efficient in data merging, a good ontology needs to have specified both what information, and how much information, is relevant to the task at hand. For example, in a system that stores data about student grades, health insurance, family income and contact address, etc, it may not be appropriate to store the ethnic background of a student. Even if it is stored in the database, it must be possible to assign it a 'relevance value' with respect to the ontology. This relevance value indicates how pertinent that field is, when, say different ontologies are merged.

In modern software development, a key phrase is "Reuse, Reuse, Reuse". In the world of ontologies, we would want to be able to create a library of reusable ontologies. This library should contain smaller, self-contained ontologies that are well separated, and coherent with respect to functionality. It would then be possible to build bigger, more powerful ontologies by merely reusing existing ontologies. In a library of ontologies, each ontology should be a consistent, self contained and closed unit. On the other hand, if each ontology is open for reuse, in which case any part of its structure can be extended as long as the original meaning is not changed, we will have been able to promote extensibility.

A truly useful and powerful ontological system should be able to constantly adapt itself, as by the combination and merger of sub-ontologies. Such intelligent systems would have the ability to deal with new data, new types of data, new types of needs and queries, and also new users. Although more powerful approaches to the development and use of ontologies are being investigated, truly dynamic ontologies do not exist yet and most current ontologies are static, or at best moderately dynamic.

Information systems with improved capabilities such as self-management could be enabled by the use of ontologies. Since they make semantics more transparent, they can be used in developing information systems with improved self-management capabilities. Self-management capabilities can include self-healing, self-protecting, self-configuring or self-optimizing [1].

3.2 An Ontology as a Classification System

An ontology can be viewed as a taxonomy implying that it is a classification system used to organize a collection of objects or entities, and impart some additional significance and meaning to the resulting categorized system. This functionality can be easily understood by analogy with the manner in which the human mind first perceives data, then recognizes and categories the data into meaningful information, and finally uses the resulting information and knowledge to make appropriate and informed decisions. An individual sees the external world, observes everything around them, and selects the items that are of relevance to a particular task in which the person is currently interested. So the ontology helps in building a personalized local model of the real world. Figure 3 shows how an ontology can help in building a model of a domain of interest in the real world.

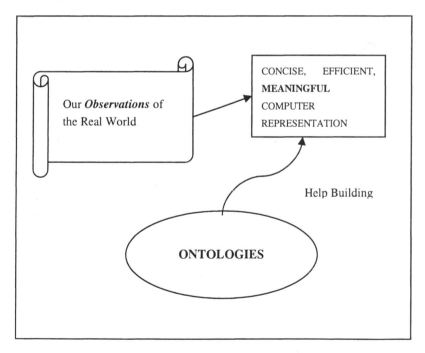

Figure1-3. How an Ontology Maps Observations to Meaningful Computer Representation

3.3   Ontologies and the Semantic Web

The *Semantic Web* is the next step in the evolution of the Internet and the World Wide Web in which ontologies will help to carry out ever more intelligent tasks on behalf of users. Indeed the idea of ontologies has almost become synonymous with the semantic web.

Figure 4 shows the architecture of the semantic web, and where ontologies are functionally positioned [1].

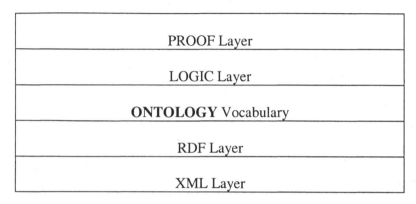

PROOF Layer
LOGIC Layer
ONTOLOGY Vocabulary
RDF Layer
XML Layer

Figure 1- 4. Architecture of the Semantic Web.

The role of each layer in the figure is briefly explained below:

1) The XML (eXtensible Markup Language) layer represents the structure of the actual data.
2) The RDF   (Resource Document Format) layer provides a representation of the meaning of data [5]
3) The Ontology vocabulary represents the common agreement about the meaning of data, which is essential for interoperability.
4) The Logic layer enables intelligent reasoning with meaningful data.
5) The Proof layer supports the exchange of proofs in inter-agent communication, enabling common understanding of how the desired information is derived.

In a   typical case of a semantic web application we observe the following characteristics that must be considered for the development of an architecture.:

1) The data is geographically distributed

2) The data has diverse ownerships

3) The data is heterogeneous (and from the real world)

4) The application must assume an open world, i.e. the information is never complete

5) The application must use some formal description of the data's meaning.

Hence we can see that ontologies make the semantic web a realizable goal and it is the semantic web that can bring the world wide web to its full potential. Ontologies have the potential to provide a qualitatively new level of services, i.e., services not realized before. such as justification, verification and gap analysis [1]. Ontologies not only define information, but also add expressiveness and reasoning capabilities.

The creation of powerful ontologies requires a deep understanding of the problem space. We need to understand the relationships between objects of interest, their co-relation and their interdependencies. So we need to clearly and unambiguously establish the relationships between various objects. The semantics (meanings) of these relationships are also important and an ontology should offer insights and facilitate knowledge management.

Two important technologies for building the semantic web – XML and RDF – are already in place.. However XML is a much more mature technology than ontologies in terms of the size of the user community, availability of support tools and viability of business models relying on the technology. It has been observed that XML is used for complexity reduction, while ontologies are used for uncertainty reduction [2].

Recall that HTML (**H**yper **T**ext **M**arkup Language) is the language utilized to encode web pages in a standard format. HTML deals with syntax, i.e. it ensures that the correct form and format are followed and so concerns itself only with the formatting of text and graphics for the user. It is a language with which web browsers specify a web page's format, but is not intended to help locate specific data on a page. Because most web pages are currently written in HTML, extracting data is a complicated task.

XML was created as a standard for online data interchange and can promote interoperability and data integration. A good one-line definition of XML is: "XML is a flexible way to create *"self-describing data"*--and to share both the format and the data on the World Wide Web, intranets, and elsewhere." [9]

However, as the amount of information on the web is growing exponentially, ways to effectively extract meaningful information from the vast amounts of data must be developed. This can be done by adding semantics (meanings) to the valid syntactic entities as can be provided by technologies such as Resource Description Framework and ontology description languages like OWL (Web Ontology Language) where OWL has additional expression power. There is a fine balance between the expressive power of these languages and the complexity (efficiency) of operations in these languages. The key is to maximize the expressive power while maintaining an acceptable performance. What XML is for syntax, RDF is for semantics. Essentially, RDF is a clear set of rules for providing descriptive information, i.e., a standard way to make simple descriptions.

Finally the W3C, the World Wide Web Consortium is a group of about 370 international companies working to develop web standards [7, 8]. To quote Tim Berners Lee, the inventor of the Web, "W3C is where the future of the web is".

4. CONCLUSION

Clearly, ontologies are a powerful tool in harnessing the true power of the Internet. Ontologies provide a high level, expressive, conceptual modeling approach for describing knowledge. When ontologies are merged, they make heterogeneous information systems interoperable. By unearthing possibly hidden relationships, ontologies facilitate the extraction of implicit design decisions and assumptions.

By their very nature, ontologies not only define information, but also add expressiveness and reasoning capabilities to a knowledge system. They provide a qualitatively new level of services. Some examples of these services are justification, verification and gap analysis [1]. Ontologies weave together a large network of human knowledge, and they complement this knowledge with machine processability.

An ontology defines the terms used to describe and represent an area of knowledge. Ontologies are used by people, databases and applications that need to share information specific to a subject or domain and encode knowledge in a domain, and across domains..

The Semantic Web is the next step in the Internet's evolution, and the development of ontologies and ontology merging techniques unleashes, harnesses, revitalizes and rejuvenates the full power of the Internet. Ontologies promote on-demand computing, and make the Semantic Web a realizable goal.

5. ACKNOWLEDGEMENTS

The authors would like to thank the Naval Research Laboratory's Base Program, Program Element No. 0602435N for sponsoring this research.

6.   REFERENCES

1. L. Stojanovic, J. Schneider, A. Maedche, S.Libischer, R. Studer, T. Lumpp, A. Abecker, G.Breiter, J. Dinger, "The Role of Ontologies in Autonomic Computing Systems", *IBM Systems Journal*, Vol 43, No 3, pp 598-616, 2004

2. C. Holsapple, K Joshi, "A Collaborative Approach to Ontology Design", *Comm. of the ACM*, February 2002, Vol 45, No 2, pp 42-47

3. H. Kim, "Predicting How Ontologies for the Semantic Web Will Evolve", *Comm. of the ACM*, February 2002, Vol 45, No 2, pp 48-54

4. N. Shadbolt, N. Gibbins, H. Glaser, S. Harris, M.Schraefel, "CS AKTive Space, or How We Learned to Stop Worrying and Love the Sematic Web", *IEEE Intelligent Systems*, Vol 19, No 3, pp 41-47, May/June 2004

5. H. Stuckenschmidt, F. van Harmelen, A. de Waard,T. Scerri, R. Bhogal, J. van Buel, I. Crowlesmith, C.Fluit, A. Kampman, J. Broekstra, E. van Mulligen, "Exploring Large Document Repositories with RDF Technology: The DOPE Project", *IEEE Intelligent Systems* Vol 19, No 3, pp 34-40, May/June 2004

6. S. Hubner, R. Spittel, U. Visser, T Vogele,., "Ontology-Based Search for Interactive Digital Maps", *IEEE Intelligent Systems*, Vol 19, No 3, pp 80-86, May/June 2004

7. Eric Miller, "The W3C's Semantic Web Activity : An Update", *IEEE Intelligent Systems*, Vol 19, No 3, pp 95-96, May/June 2004

8. URL for more detail on The World Wide Web Consortium:http://www.w3.org/

9. To Learn more about XML: http://www.oreilly.com/catalog/learnxml/

Chapter 2

WEB SERVICES OVERVIEW FOR NET-CENTRIC OPERATIONS

Elizabeth Warner, Uday Katikaneni, Roy Ladner, Frederick Petry, and Kevin B. Shaw
U.S. Naval Research Laboratory, Stennis Space Center, MS 39529

Abstract: Web Services are being adopted as the enabling technology to provide net-centric capabilities for many Department of Defense (DoD) operations. The Navy Enterprise Portal, for example, is Web Services-based, and the Department of the Navy is promulgating guidance for developing Web Services. In this chapter, we provide an overview of Web Services and provide examples of the use of Web Services for net-centric operations as applied to meteorological and oceanographic (MetOc) data. We then present issues related to the Navy's use of MetOc Web Services. Finally, we describe our work on the Advanced MetOc Broker (AMB). The AMB supports a new, advanced approach to using Web Services; namely, the automated identification, retrieval and fusion of MetOc data. Systems based on this approach would not require extensive end-user application development for each new Web Service from which data can be retrieved.

Key words: Web Services, Net-Centric Warfare, Automated Reasoning, Intelligent Systems, MetOc Data

1.   INTRODUCTION

Net-centric operations for intelligence, national security and war-fighting activities broadly include the combination of emerging tactics, techniques, and procedures that a fully or even partially networked force can employ to create a decisive advantage. These net-centric capabilities work to provide information superiority in the information age.[1]

Web Services are being adopted as the enabling technology to provide net-centric capabilities for many Department of Defense (DoD) operations.

The Navy Enterprise Portal (NEP), for example, is Web Services-based, and the Department of the Navy is promulgating guidance for developing Web Services. Web Services technology is rapidly being adopted, leading to an ever-increasing number of data providers offering data via new Web Services. Rapidly integrating applications with these new Web Services is significant to maintaining information superiority in a network-centric world.

Web Services make interoperability for client and server applications easier to achieve; however, Web Services technology has not eliminated the need for humans to develop client code to connect to each Web Service. While this subject has been brought up in the commercial context of the automated Web[2], it has not been fully addressed in the Navy context of meteorological and oceanographic (MetOc) data. Since Web Services give the promise of discoverable, self-describing services that stick to common standards, their employ should allow the possibility of more efficient application integration.

One means of minimizing the development of new client code for each Web Service to be invoked is the Joint MetOc Broker Language (JMBL). JMBL enables one jointly agreed upon Web Service to foster DoD wide MetOc data retrieval interoperability. Another means for minimizing development of new client code might be to allow for disparate Web Services and to automate application development using knowledge based techniques and intelligent machine reasoning.

In this chapter, we provide an overview of Web Services and provide examples of the use of Web Services for Navy net-centric operations as applied to MetOc data. We then present issues related to the Navy's use of MetOc Web Services. Finally, we describe our work on the Advanced MetOc Broker (AMB). The AMB supports a new, advanced approach to the use of Web Services; namely, the automated identification, retrieval and fusion of MetOc data. Systems based on this approach would not require extensive client application development for each new Web Service from which data can be retrieved.

2.   WEB SERVICES OVERVIEW

Web Services provide data and services to users and applications over the Internet through a consistent set of standards and protocols. The most commonly used standards and protocols include, but are not necessarily limited to, the Extensible Markup Language (XML), Simple Object Access Protocol (SOAP), the Web Services Definition Language (WSDL) and Universal Discovery Description and Integration (UDDI).

XML is a language used to define data in a platform and programming language independent manner. XML has become one of the widely used standards in interoperable exchange of data on the Internet but does not define the semantics of the data it describes. Instead, the semantics of an XML document are defined by the applications that process them.

XML Schemas define the structure or building blocks of an XML document. Some of these structures include the elements and attributes, the hierarchy and number of occurrences of elements, and data types, among others.[3]

WSDL allows the creation of XML documents that define the "contract" for a Web Service. The "contract" details the acceptable requests that will be honored by the Web Service and the types of responses that will be generated.[4] The "contract" also defines the XML messaging mechanism of the service. The messaging mechanism, for example, may be specified as SOAP.

A UDDI registry provides a way for data providers to advertise their Web Services and for consumers to find data providers and desired services. Data provided about a Web Service can be categorized much like information in a telephone book into "white" pages, "yellow" pages and, unlike a telephone book, the "green" pages. The white pages include basic provider information such as name, address, business description and contact information. The yellow pages provide services listed by category as determined by the American Industry Classification System and the Standard Industrial Classification. The white and yellow pages include enough information for a consumer to determine whether they need the technical specification for the service, which is contained in the green pages. The green pages may either contain or point to the WSDL file. An interface to a UDDI registry, may allow users to search for Web Services by business category, business name or service. [2]

It is, of course, not necessary to register a Web Service with a UDDI registry. However, that would be similar to a business not listing its telephone number in a telephone directory. Not having a listing would make it more difficult for consumers to discover and utilize a Web Service. This advertisement of Web Services may or may not be desirable for net-centric operations in the DoD community.

A graphic representation of the Web Services protocol stack [2] as described above is shown in Figure 1. A Web Service describes its interface with a WSDL file and may be registered in a UDDI registry. Interfaces defined in XML often identify SOAP as the required XML messaging protocol. SOAP allows for the exchange of information between computers regardless of platform or language.

A sample use of the protocol stack is illustrated in Figure 2. In Figure 2, a Web Service publishes its existence with one or more UDDI registries. Next, a user discovers the service from a UDDI registry and retrieves a description of the service. The user then either automatically invokes the service or writes an application that invokes the service by sending an XML message over the specified transport to the service. The Web Service then returns an XML message over the specified transport.

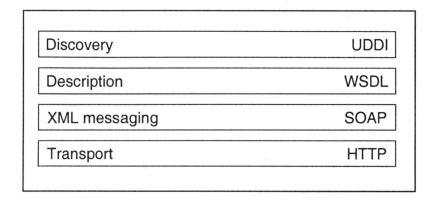

Figure 2-1. Web Services Protocol Stack.

There are applications that provide services on the Web without using all components of the Web Services protocol stack described above. These Web-based services employ diverse methods for discovery, description, messaging and transport. Within these Web-based services adherence to standards and protocols vary.

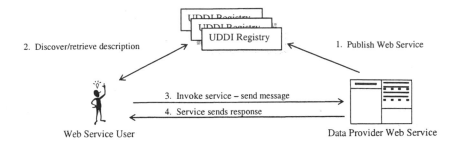

Figure 2-2. Illustrated Use of Web Services

3. EXAMPLES OF WEB SERVICES WITHIN THE METOC COMMUNITY

The intent of net-centric operations is to equip intelligence agencies, national security groups and warfighters with dramatically improved capabilities for sharing, accessing, and exchanging data. This improved capability is intended to provide a significant advantage over opposing forces that are not networked, or are less networked than U.S. forces.[1] Our concentration in net-centric operations is focused on improving delivery of MetOc data to Naval warfighters in order to achieve this information superiority. Following are some of the architectures using Web Services and Web-based services to accomplish this goal.

3.1 Navy Enterprise Portal

The Navy Enterprise Portal (NEP) is a Web Service access portal that is provided by the Department of the Navy. The NEP makes a distinction between user-interfaces and data services. It does this by allowing for a User Facing Service that operates in a Web-browser and which interacts with a Data Oriented Service on a remote server. A Data Oriented Service is not tightly coupled to any client application. The NEP allows the user to simultaneously access multiple User Facing Services from the same Web-browser interface.[5]

3.2 Geospatial Information DataBase (GIDB™)

The Geospatial Information DataBase (GIDB™) System is an example of a Web-based service that invokes Web Services. The GIDB is an object-oriented digital mapping portal system designed by the Digital Mapping, Charting and Geodesy Analysis Program of the Naval Research Laboratory. Development of the system began in 1994.[6] The GIDB currently connects users to over 500 servers offering over 2,500 services.

The GIDB's communications gateway allows users to obtain data from a wide variety of data providers distributed over the Internet. The GIDB System uses XML technologies to obtain data from data providers who offer an XML-based interface.[7] Not all data providers distribute data via Web Services. For those data providers who are Web-based data providers rather than Web Services data providers, the GIDB uses the data provider's interface of choice. This may be a native API or other mechanism.

The data providers accessible through the GIDB include such diverse entities as Fleet Numerical Meteorology and Oceanography Center (FNMOC), the U.S. Geological Survey, Digital Earth/NASA, and the Geography Network/ESRI. A significant FNMOC product is the Coupled Ocean/Atmosphere Mesoscale Prediction System (COAMPS) data. The atmospheric components of COAMPS are used operationally by the US Navy for short-term numerical weather prediction for various regions around the world. The GIDB's communications gateway provides a convenient means for users to obtain COAMPS data and incorporate it with other vector and raster data in map form. The GIDB establishes a well-defined interface that brings together such heterogeneous data for a common geo-referenced presentation to the user.

The GIDB user display includes the capability for 3D terrain visualizations with map overlay.[8] Research has also been conducted into extending the GIDB to use spatio-temporal data mining techniques for Naval planning applications.[9,10,11] An illustration of the current application interface for a data request is shown in Figure 3. This picture shows the fusion of forecast data with such features as marine minerals and coordinate reference lines.

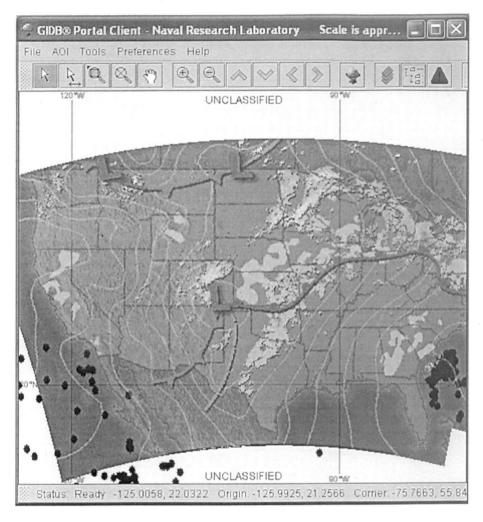

Figure 2-3. GIDB Data Fusion Over the Internet

3.3 Joint MetOc Broker Language (JMBL)

The Joint MetOc Broker Language (JMBL) is a specification for a standard language to be used in MetOc Web Services to broker the exchange of information between MetOc data providers and user applications. JMBL does not define a data model, but simply a syntax that allows standardized request and response structures for MetOc data queries. A moving factor in the creation of JMBL was a need to move beyond having distinct interfaces for every possible combination of user application systems and data provider systems. JMBL was developed with input from joint forces including Army,

Navy, Air Force, etc. The goal of JMBL was to define one Web Service based on jointly defined XML Schemas that would serve all types of MetOc data requests. Each agency would implement this jointly defined Web Service and would therefore have interoperable implementations of the same Web Service.

The JMBL Web Service is defined by one WSDL file and several XML Schemas. These Schemas define the structure of requests that the JMBL Web Service will accept and the structure of responses that the JMBL Web Service will provide. The request and response Schemas include several other Schemas, which define global data types and structures. Figure 4 shows this conceptual organization. As shown in Figure 4, several of the global Schemas are included in other global Schemas. Schemas in Figure 4 are represented by "XSD".

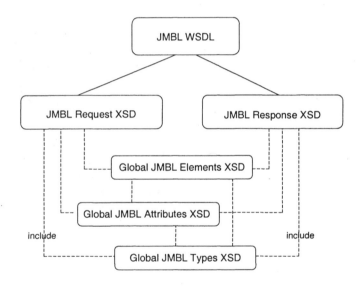

Figure 2-4. Conceptual View of JMBL WSDL and Schemas

3.4   Tactical Environmental Data Services (TEDServices)

The Navy's Tactical Environmental Data Services (TEDServices) is a new, scaleable and modular environmental data repository, designed to support Warfighters, Weapon Systems, and MetOc data users. TEDServices is currently an example of a distributed Web-based service that defines its interface in Java and uses the HTTP transport protocol. TEDServices is currently capable of interfacing with JMBL based Web Services to obtain data. Work is underway to integrate other JMBL capabilities into TEDServices. This would allow users to interact with TEDServices servers via JMBL requests.

TEDServices includes a middleware infrastructure that enables the data transport between nodes in the system (Figure 5). This figure illustrates the distributed nature of TEDServices. Each node is a Web server, which autonomously communicates with other nodes to achieve its objectives.

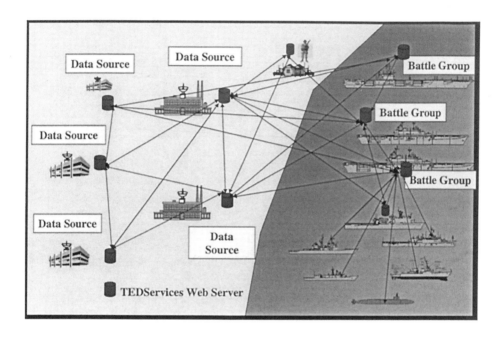

Figure 2-5. TEDServices Distributed Web Server Topology

A focus of TEDServices is the active management of bandwidth and data. Data updates are continuously transmitted to end-user environments and are pre-staged in a local data cache until cancelled expressly by users or cancelled by the server due to non-use by end-users. This greatly reduces end-user retrieval times for large data sets. TEDServices combines the concepts of shared data spaces with Web-based services as shown in Figure 6. This figure shows the conceptual installation of a TEDServices Web server on a Navy platform in the ship's OA (weather) Division. All users on the platform have access to the Web server and data pre-staged there. Off-board users have similar access.

Large scale data transfer can be difficult when network communications are unstable. TEDServices employs Resumable Object Streams (ROS) for all data traffic between TEDServices Web servers across the network to achieve fail-safe data transportation under these conditions.   ROS allows either the client or server side of a request to lose network connection, regain it, and have the request continue where it left off.   Retransmission of the previously transmitted portion is not necessary in either case.   Data requests can still be wrapped in compression and/or encryption.   The ROS transmission controls add almost no bandwidth overhead to the communication (approximately 13 bytes).

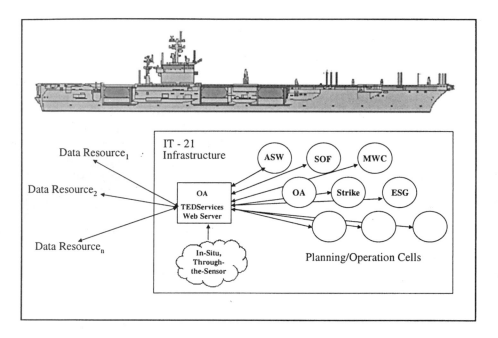

Figure 2-6. Conceptual Installation of a TEDServices Server

In addition to ROS, TEDServices uses an advanced data compression scheme (LPAC).   LPAC provides higher lossless compression ratios than data compression methods currently favored by MetOc data users for large gridded data sets.   Data is compressed prior to network transmission.   It is also stored in the compressed format and uncompressed only on extraction to end-users.   A Java-implementation of spatial DataBlade type functionality was transitioned to TEDServices by Barrodale Computing Services (BCS), under the direction of the MetOc Systems Program Office to provide the methods for complex extractions from these datasets.[11,12]   ROS and LPAC take into account the special needs of sea-going Navy Web-based clients who require large chunks of MetOc data on frequent intervals over tenuous communications with limited bandwidth.

TEDServices represents the type of client/server network topology that is important in many net-centric operations. Instead of many clients connecting to a single server, TEDServices enables many clients to connect to many servers in a many-to-many topology, as previously illustrated in Figure 5. In this many-to-many topology Web servers can act as clients to other Web servers.

4. NAVY ISSUES FOR METOC NET-CENTRIC OPERATIONS

The Web Services and Web-based services described above each contribute to the Navy's goal of information superiority in a network-centric world. Use of Web Services and Web-based services as described in this paper is not necessarily without pitfalls. Even with the advent of Web Services and Web-based services, human resources are still required to integrate these data sources into applications. Compatibility of XML Schema versions is an inherent issue, and Web Services based on common XML Schemas may be implemented in a manner to create inconsistent results. Some examples are described below.

GIDB, for example, does not automatically discover new Web Services or Web-based data services. A human in the loop is necessary to find relevant data on the Internet and write application code to connect the GIDB Portal System to the data source. The GIDB currently connects to over 500 servers offering over 2,500 services. The fact that some of the code used to connect to these servers is common to multiple servers helps with code development and maintenance.

While GIDB establishes a single portal to multiple servers, JMBL seeks to establish a uniform Web Service that that can be separately implemented by multiple data providers. JMBL seeks to accomplish this through adoption of a specified XML Schema and WSDL. Our experience has been, however, that the implementation of the Web Service by different data providers can create the likelihood of varying implementations that may impact interoperability. In these cases, client side code that conforms to the particular implementation must be developed. Case in point, service providers can choose to implement as much or as little of the JMBL Schema as they wish. The XML Schema, for example, allows users to request data that has been modified since a specified date and time. While one service provider supports data responses to this request, another service provider returns an error message. Although both providers produce gridded numerical forecast model output on a scheduled timetable, the provider producing the error message does not believe that any users would request its data in that manner.

As the use of JMBL increases, a means for client applications to elegantly address Schema version compatibilities and Schema enhancements may be needed. The JMBL v. 3.0 Schema, for example, is not backward compatible with earlier versions. A client side request that conforms to v. 3.0 would not be considered a valid request to a Web Service that has implemented JMBL v. 2.19. Similarly, a client side request that conforms to JMBL v. 2.19 may not be considered a valid request to a Web Service that has implemented JMBL v. 3.0. Conforming client side code is necessary for each non-backward compatible version of the Schema that is implemented by each JMBL based Web Service. Any client application interfacing with more than one implementation of a JMBL based Web Service must contain code capable of interacting with each JMBL version.

A similar need exists for resolving semantic and business rule differences that result from specific implementations. While, as described above, JMBL defines a syntax that allows standardization of terms used to request MetOc information and respond to such requests, the semantics are not tightly defined. JMBL Web Service implementers are free to each implement a different sub-set of JMBL and each may interpret various JMBL elements and attributes in incompatible ways. Work is underway to produce a set of conventions and JMBL modifications that will reduce this ambiguity.

As previously mentioned, there is a need to generate client code that connects to Web Services. Several tools exist to automatically generate client side code from WSDL and/or to execute publicly available methods on the Web Service. This certainly helps to streamline the integration process and cut down on the amount of required human resources, but all of the existing tools do not necessarily achieve automated integration. We have used Axis v. 1.1, for example, with JMBL v. 2.19 and v. 3.0. In these cases, Axis v. 1.1 was not able to handle several features of the XML Schema. Figure 4 shows the interrelation of these JMBL Schemas. While JMBL includes global Schemas in the request and response Schemas, the global Schemas are not assigned individual name spaces. The JMBL elements are therefore unqualified. Axis v. 1.1 does not recognize unqualified elements and consequently generates client side Java code that produces invalid instances of the JMBL Schemas.

There are also issues with Axis v. 1.1 correctly producing Java code for several "choice" elements illustrated in Figure 7. Axis v. 1.1 is not sufficiently flexible to handle all possible design choices allowed by XML Schema developers. In particular, JMBL 3.0 defines "GriddedAnalysisForecast" and "GriddedClimatology" as empty elements, i.e., they have no attributes and do not have a type (string, integer, etc.).

Axis does not generate classes for these elements, leading to invalid instances of XML generated by the Java classes that Axis does make.

```
<xsd:choice>
    <xsd:element ref="GriddedAnalysisForecast" />
    <xsd:element ref="GriddedClimatology" />
</xsd:choice>
```

Figure 2-7. Sample JMBL Choice Elements

Unlike JMBL, TEDServices provides a uniform implementation of its services. TEDServices does not automatically discover new Web-based data servers. Additionally, application development is necessary for TEDServices to obtain new data formats from new data providers.

5.   OBSERVATION AND FUTURE DIRECTION

Web Services play a significant role in net-centric operations for intelligence, national security and war-fighting applications. We have discussed the use and implementation of Web Services within the Navy and have presented specific examples from the MetOc community. We have also presented issues that have arisen within each of these examples. Web Services merely constitute a baseline specification that provides the foundation on which users, under current approaches, write specialized client applications in order to retrieve data over the Internet. The number of specialized client applications and the amount of application development time increases dramatically as the number of different available Web Services and Web-based applications increase.

While the use of XML in Web Services promotes the loose coupling of client and server applications in a language independent manner, application development is still tied to the semantics of each specific Web Service. In addition to application development time, non-developer time may be incurred in the formulation and adoption of a single Schema that will be implemented by multiple DoD agencies. Resolution of semantic differences are being addressed by the development of ontologies with languages such as OWL.[13]

Further research is needed in order to effectively leverage the many Web Services that will be available as time progresses. Currently we are developing the Advanced MetOc Broker (AMB) that could be used in systems to overcome the semantic limitations inherent to MetOc Web Services. The AMB could be used to identify, retrieve and integrate relevant environmental data, particularly MetOc data, from new and ad hoc Web Services. The AMB is being developed to apply MetOc ontologies and knowledge-based techniques to meteorological and oceanographic forms of data to support a new, advanced approach to the use of Web Services; namely, the automated identification, retrieval and fusion of MetOc data.[14,15,16]. This methodology could be extended beyond the MetOc domain to other domains. Systems based on this approach would not require extensive end-user application development for each Web Service from which data can be retrieved.

6.   ACKNOWLEDGEMENTS

The authors would like to thank the Naval Research Laboratory's Base Program, Program Element No. 0602435N for sponsoring this research.

7.   REFERENCES

1. Network-Centric Warfare Creating a Decisive Warfighting Advantage, 2003, Director, Force Transformation, Office of the Secretary of Defense, 1000 Defense, Pentagon, Washington, DC 20301-1000, December 2003.
2. Cerami, E., 2002, *Web Services Essentials*, O'Reilly and Associates, 2002.
3. XML Schema Tutorial, 2004, http://www.w3schools.com/schema.
4. Web Services Definition Language, 2004, http://www.perfectxml.com/WebSvc3.asp.
5. Navy Enterprise Portal (2004); https://portal.tfw.navy.mil, http://agendas.ca.com/ agendas/SessionDetails.asp?SessionId=1595,http://ams.confex.com/ams /Annual2005/techprogram/paper_86973.htm
6. Chung, M., Cobb, M., Shaw, K., Arctur, D., 1995, An object-oriented approach for handling topology in vpf products, *GIS/LIS'95 Proceedings*, 1:14-16.
7. Wilson, R., M. Cobb, F. McCreedy, R. Ladner, D. Olivier, T. Lovitt, K. Shaw, F. Petry, M. Abdelguerfi, 2003, Geographical Data Interchange Using XML-Enabled Technology within the GIDB System in *XML Data Management*, A. B. Chaudhri, ed., Addison-Wesley, 353-374.
8. Ladner R., Abdelguerfi, M., Shaw, K., 2000, 3d mapping of an interactive synthetic environment, *IEEE Computer*, 33(3): 35-39.
9. Ladner, R., Petry, F., 2002, Assessment of spatial data mining Tools for integration into an object-oriented GIS (GIDB), *Proc. 13ᵗʰ Int. Conference Database and Expert Systems Applications*, 113-122.
10. Ladner, R., Petry, F., 2002, Spatio-temporal data mining and knowledge discovery: issues overview in *Mining Spatio-Temporal Information Systems*, Abdelguerfi, M. and Ladner R. eds., Kluwer , pp. 1-19.

11. Warner, E., Ladner, R., Petry, F. and Shea, J., 2004, Advanced Techniques in Delivering Data to the Warfighter in a Distributed Information System, *Proc. SPIE Defense & Security Symposium*, 753-761.
12. Katikaneni, U., Ladner, R. and Petry, F., 2004, Internet delivery of meteorological and oceanographic data in wide area naval usage environments, *WWW2004 proceedings*, 84-88.
13. Paolucci, M. and Sycara, K, 2003, Autonomous semantic web services, *IEEE Internet Computing*, 12: 34-41.
14. Alameh, N., 2003, Chaining geographic information web services, *IEEE Internet Computing*, 12:22-29.
15. Fonseca, F., Egenhofer, M., Agouris, P. and Camara, G., 2002, Using ontologies for integrated geographic information systems, *Transactions in GIS*, 6(3): 47-61.
16. Fonseca, F. and Davis, C., 1999, Using the internet to access geographic information, in *Interoperating GIS*, Eds, M. Goodchild, M. Egenhofer, R. Fegeas and C. Kottman, eds., Kluwer Pub., Norwell MA, pp. 313-324.

Chapter 3

METADATA CONCEPTS TO SUPPORT A NET-CENTRIC DATA ENVIRONMENT

Kenneth J. Laskey·

The MITRE Corporation, 7515 Colshire Drive, McLean VA 22102

Abstract: The term *metadata* is often defined as "data about data" but that circular reference does little to describe what constitutes metadata and how it is used. Here, we will focus on metadata as conceived to support the concepts of a service-oriented architecture and, in particular, as it relates to the DoD Net-Centric Data Strategy and the NCES core services; more specifically, what types and structure of metadata are implied by current use cases, what functions are implied to support creating, maintaining, and using such metadata, and what is implied about a metadata infrastructure that would support such metadata and its related functions.

Key words: metadata, service-oriented architecture, net-centric, GIG ES, GES, NCES

1.   INTRODUCTION

Use of the term *metadata* has expanded beyond the point of conveying a definitive meaning when the word is used. The data model in a database is traditionally looked at as metadata because it describes the structure of the database. Similarly, information included before a table in a data file can identify the variables represented by the values in the rows and columns, and this is often described as metadata.

When used in the context of a service-oriented architecture (SOA), metadata typically serves a much wider purpose. For the myriad of capabilities with which metadata has been connected in an SOA context, it

---

·The author's affiliation with The MITRE Corporation is provided for identification purposes only, and is not intended to convey or imply MITRE's concurrence with, or support for, the positions, opinions or viewpoints expressed by the author.

would be more accurately described as that subset of the data related to an entity that provides some critical descriptive information which is especially useful in some context for identifying, using, or otherwise interacting with the entity. Context is especially important. The entity may be a physical object or a computational object, such as a data set or an application, or anything else to which there is a need to apply a description. Any subset of data (*i.e.*, any information associated with or comprising the entity) may be identified as metadata if it satisfies the needs for some context, and there may be multiple metadata sets corresponding to any number of contexts.

Admittedly, this is quite an expansion over the traditional use of the term. As an example of the expanded use for different contexts, consider the ways in which metadata for a book may be defined and used. For a librarian, the Library of Congress classification number is likely an important metadata element. Conversely, for a bookseller, the classification number is not likely to be as important but the current sales price would be (while this price may not be of interest to the librarian). The text in the book is unlikely to be identified as metadata, but specific quotes from the book may be metadata for someone advertising the book.

2.   CONSIDERATIONS FOR NET-CENTRICITY

The Global Information Grid (GIG) Core Enterprise Services (CES) Strategy [1] calls for "robust [GIG] enterprise services (GES) [to] provide visibility and access to data, enabling the end user to execute an intelligent pull of mission-tailored information from anywhere within the network environment." Moreover, "the CESs provide the basic ability to search the DoD enterprise for desired information and services, and then establish a connection to the desired service/data."

This vision describes an environment where the interaction between the providers and consumers of resources must be flexible and readily configurable across entities (consumers, providers, and resources) that had no previous knowledge that the others existed. This implies a number of capabilities that go beyond the traditional data and processing paradigm.

- Consumers must be able to search for resources without knowing the details, such as specific APIs, of the resource beforehand. This implies that the description of the resource must be expressed in a universally accessible format and, though it will be associated with the resource, the description will be external to the resource so it can be accessed without reading or otherwise invoking the resource itself.
- The external description must contain sufficient detail so the consumer can decide if the resource will satisfy the current need.

- If the resource is appropriate, the consumer must be able to access the resource content or invoke the resource processing without previously knowing the APIs or other details of the resource.
- If the consumer attempts to access the resource, sufficient information must be available about the consumer so that the provider or an agent acting for the provider can determine if the access is authorized.
- The producer and consumer must share a common format for the description <u>and</u> must also agree on how to interpret the description content. This may be accomplished by indicating a common vocabulary or distinct vocabularies for which services exist to mediate a translation.

The DoD Net-Centric Data Strategy [2] lays out a path for accomplishing this through the use of metadata. As a notional example of metadata enabling net-centric capabilities, consider a user looking for meteorological data in Afghanistan. Metadata associated with a data resource that could support this includes

1. general document metadata with the name of the data resource and the geographic locations from where it can be accessed; metadata specific to the function of the data resource, such as the date, time, and geographic location where the data was collected,
2. access control restrictions which must be satisfied (or possibly licensing terms if it is a commercial source) and a pointer to the service interface (*e.g.* WSDL [3]) to retrieve the data,
3. a pointer to pedigree information describing the quality of the data as evaluated based on how the data was collected and processed and the accuracy of the measurements.

The request for the meteorological data may generate a log file detailing the services invoked and resources used to satisfy the request, and the log file could be archived using a network storage service. Associated with the stored log would be metadata containing a log ID, the date of the request, and the identity of the requester. Note, in this example, the log file itself is not considered metadata but information describing the log file is. A pointer to the log metadata would be returned with the requested data so the requester would both know how the request was fulfilled and be able to point to the log as a repeatable means to satisfy a similar request in the future.

In this example, the distinction between what is only data (the log file) and what is data used as metadata (*e.g.*, when the log file was created) is unimportant (and is likely to change in other contexts). What is important is that subsets of the information space surrounding the meteorological data were available as needed for various services in order to locate, access, and evaluate the suitability of the resource before the resource was ever used. In fact, using the resource was possible because metadata could directly supply or point to information that the service needed to complete its function. This is the role played by metadata in a service-oriented architecture and the context for the present discussion.

3. DEFINITION OF METADATA

To support and enable the capabilities required of a service-oriented architecture and the GIG CES vision of net-centricity, we offer the following definition:

Metadata is that set of descriptive properties which serves one or more of the following functions
1. uniquely characterizes an entity and for which values associated with the descriptive properties allow a user (human or machine) to discriminate between one entity and another,
2. describes how the entity and its contents can be accessed (both procedurally and the terms of access) in either a read or write mode or executed if the entity comprises processing instructions,
3. contains pointers to information not explicitly part of a given metadata set but which is required as processing or control inputs by other applications or services.

Metadata often includes what the entity is, where it is located, and how to make use of it. It may describe entity properties such as format, structure/organization, context, business rules, or any other chosen elements of its integral or associated data or capabilities. It may include the calling argument to methods, invocation of services, or similar executable commands that act on the content of an instance of the entity, including accessing it from its native storage format.

As noted in both the book example in the Introduction and the weather example in the previous section, what constitutes the appropriate metadata set depends on the context of the user and the current needs to be satisfied. Thus, it is less important to have defined the perfect metadata set than to ensure that the combined metadata available can provide or support access to the critical information at the critical time.

4. NET-CENTRIC EFFORTS TO IDENTIFY METADATA CONTENT

As noted in the previous section, what constitutes metadata can be quite variable and the only real test to see if one has the "right" set of metadata is to ask whether that set satisfies the task at hand. To provide more structure to the description of metadata, numerous efforts have attempted to organize metadata into classes, sometimes forming a metadata taxonomy. This section will look at several such efforts that are particularly relevant to GIG Enterprise Services. Later sections will discuss specific results from one of the efforts and will attempt to provide some clarity as to how a consolidated view of these efforts support the operational needs of GES and the net-centric vision.

4.1   DoD Net-Centric Data Strategy perspective

The DoD Net-Centric Data Strategy describes the DoD data vision and specifically, the Net-Centric Data Goals. These goals are listed in Table 3-1.

Table 3-1. DoD Net-Centric Data Goals

Goals that increase data that is available to communities and the Enterprise
• **visibility**: descriptive metadata about the data asset has been provided to a catalog that is visible to the Enterprise
• **accessibility**: data is stored such that users and applications in the Enterprise can access it
• **institutionalizing**: data approaches are incorporated into DoD processes and practices
Goals that ensure data is usable by both anticipated and unanticipated users and applications
• **understandability**: through strong emphasis on Community of Interest (COI)-level consensus as made visible through various DDMS (DoD Discovery Metadata Standard) metadata
• **trustworthiness**: through mechanisms such as providing defined pedigree and security information and then having COI mark what is "authoritative"
• **interoperability**: resulting from compliance with metadata standards (i.e., DDMS) and data exposure standards (e.g., GES discovery interface standards)
• **responsiveness to users**: perspective of users through involvement in COIs and evaluating data sources, catalogs, or services, and content metadata usability

In discussing the goals, the Data Strategy alludes to but does not further define the following classes of metadata:

- *Structural*: how data assets are physically composed (*e.g.* type of file: GIF, JPEG, ...) and relationships between specific parts of the data asset
- *Discovery*: key attributes and concepts of a data asset used for discovery; this includes the means to enable a user to discriminate between individual elements of a data asset or across data assets
- *Service*: defines the capabilities of the service, the necessary inputs to use the service, and a description of what the service provides
- *Content*: provides topics, keywords, context, and other content-related information to give users and applications (including search engines) insight into the meaning and context of the data
- *Security*: information (*e.g.*, security and privacy markings consistent with applicable standards) through which systems will be able to control access to assets based on *classification metadata* and enable typically

inaccessible assets to be available to users and applications that have appropriate access needs

- *Pedigree*: allow for identification of the author, publisher, and sources contributing to the data, allowing users and applications to assess the derivation of the data
- *Other*: vocabularies, taxonomic structures used for organizing data assets, interface specifications, mapping tables, ...

4.2   DDMS perspective

The DoD Discovery Metadata Standard (DDMS) [4] was developed as a standard to support the net-centric goal of visibility across the Department of Defense. Its intent is to establish a common specification for the description of data assets[1] and thus enable the capability to locate all data assets across the Enterprise[2], regardless of format, type, location, or classification.   To facilitate data asset discovery, DDMS is developed as a common set of descriptive metadata elements, including a core set that is identified as mandatory to enable a basic level of visibility.

The DDMS logical model contains a core layer as defined in the specification and an extensible layer intended to support domain-specific or Community of Interest discovery metadata requirements. The core layer is composed of four category sets:

- *Security Category Set*: describes security classification and related fields needed to support access control, but not intended to support comprehensive resource security marking; the Net-Centric Data Strategy directly references this category set in describing its security metadata
- *Resource Category Set*: describes aspects of a data asset that support maintenance, administration, and pedigree of the data asset; the Net-Centric Data Strategy directly references this category set in describing its pedigree metadata
- *Summary Content Category Set*: describes concepts and additional contextual aspects of the data asset and is intended to aid in precision discovery; the Net-Centric Data Strategy directly references this category set in describing its content metadata
- *Format Category Set*: describes physical attributes of the data asset, including elements such as file size, bit-rate or frame rate, and MIME type; the Net-Centric Data Strategy directly references this category set in describing its format/structural metadata

---

[1] The DOD Net-Centric Data Strategy defines a *data asset* as any entity that is composed of data. The DDMS considers the term to include services that provide access to data.

[2] In the DDMS context, the *Enterprise* refers to the Department of Defense, its organizations and related agencies.

A further breakdown defines *primary categories* of the core layer, each with its own set of constituent elements. The primary categories, shown in Table 3-2, are considered mandatory if they contain at least one mandatory element and are otherwise optional.

Table 3-2. DDMS Primary Category Sets

Core Layer Category Set	Primary Category	Obligation
The *Security* elements enable the description of security classification and related fields	Security	Mandatory
	Title	Mandatory
	Identifier	Mandatory
	Creator	Mandatory
	Publisher	Optional
Resource elements enable the description of maintenance and administration information	Contributor	Optional
	Date	Optional
	Rights	Optional
	Language	Optional
	Type	Optional
	Source	Optional
	Subject	Mandatory
	Geospatial Coverage	Mandatory unless not Applicable
The *Summary Content* elements enable the description of concepts and topics	Temporal Coverage	Mandatory unless not Applicable
	Virtual Coverage	Optional
	Description	Optional
The *Format* elements enable the description of physical attributes of the asset	Format	Optional

4.3   NCES Analysis of Alternatives (AoA) Use Cases

Net-Centric Enterprise Services (NCES) is a program created to provide the services and capabilities that are key to enabling the ubiquitous access to reliable decision-quality information that is envisioned by GES. The initial scope and requirements for GES were defined through the NCES Analysis of Alternatives (AoA) [5]. In support of the AoA activity, an initial set of core enterprise services were identified and further defined by inter-Service, inter-Agency teams, and then the AoA effort defined a set of use cases corresponding to these core services, with the use cases representing typical scenarios that an early NCES deployment might support.

In addition to the AoA effort to define services, it was widely recognized that there had been no detailed presentation of what metadata must be created and managed, how it would be managed, and by whom. Thus, a subsequent effort was chartered to fill that gap by providing a concept of operations (CONOPS) for metadata. In order to provide continuity with the

work of the AoA, the metadata CONOPS effort [6] analyzed a subset of the AoA use cases (Table 3-3) to determine
- what types of metadata were implied by the use cases;
- what functions were implied if such metadata was to be created, maintained, and used;
- what was implied about a metadata infrastructure that would be needed to support this metadata and the related functions.

Table 3-3. AoA use cases analyzed for Metadata CONOPS

NCES Core Services	Corresponding Use Cases
Discovery	Generalized combination of discovery of persons, content, services, and metadata use cases
Enterprise Services Management	Integrated Service Management
Mediation	Dissemination by channel
	General data access
Messaging	E-mail
	Notification
	Mailing/distribution lists
	Newsgroups/message boards
	Instant messaging

The first stage of the analysis was to consider each step from each use case in Table 3-3 and to identify the likely metadata needed to support the step. The second stage was to look across use cases and collect the individually identified metadata into common metadata sets and then to look for further commonalities in structure and use. The full analysis considered the following points:
- a common defined purpose for the set
- notional elements that would be included in the metadata set
- other defined metadata sets that would serve as components of a composite set (discussed below)
- life cycle aspects and other points to consider about the metadata set

The analysis included one or more interviews with the relevant task lead for each core service in order to ensure an in-depth understanding of the use case details and how metadata was a part of the scenario. For some of the services, use cases were combined into a single generalized use case because the required metadata and metadata processes were the same across most or all of the use cases; this was most notably done for Discovery and, to some extent, Messaging.

Note, the intent of the metadata analysis was to be wide-ranging but not necessarily to be complete or definitive. For example, aspects of a logging function seemed to naturally arise during the analysis even though this functionality was not directly included in the use cases. Thus, logging was considered with respect to potential needs and uses of metadata, but defining full details of the logging function were out of scope for a metadata effort. Conversely, while not all of the AoA use cases were included in the analysis, the investigation followed a systematic process and covered a large enough range of metadata activities to provide insight into the demands on metadata and the systems that would support it.

It should also be noted that services described in the context of the metadata analysis, especially those beyond the core services as defined in the AoA, and the registry capabilities indicated as needed to support metadata are notional and there is no NCES commitment to build these services or to build these as described.

5.   FINDINGS FROM METADATA ANALYSIS FOR NET-CENTRIC ENTERPRISE SERVICES

The AoA use case analysis considered a select number of use cases but the results of analyzing each use case step produced a significant amount of data, making presentation of the entire metadata analysis beyond the scope of this discussion.   However, several instances of the analysis will be presented to demonstrate the process and the results.   This will lead to observations on how to categorize metadata, conclusions on the purposes specific metadata types will likely need to serve, and suggestions for infrastructure capabilities to support these metadata needs.

5.1   First stage of analysis: examining the individual AoA use case steps

The analysis of each use case step typically yielded one or more types of metadata. For example, one step of the General Data Access use case stated

Data Access Service (DAS) invokes Find Service to search repository of Data Access Methods (DAM) for candidate DAMs that can support current data request.

In the full use case, the Data Access Service is described as a single Mediation service that receives data access requests and can invoke any Data Access Method.   In turn, the DAM is a service that is specific to a given data resource and possibly the specific data requested. By design, every DAM responds to the DAS in a standard, prescribed manner, and the DAS coordinates delivery of results back to the requester.

The question is then what metadata is needed for this step to successfully occur. DAS will search a repository for candidate DAMs, thus indicating the need for DAM metadata (later combined into service metadata). From the remaining context, it is known that multiple DAMs may exist and so the DAM metadata must include information (some expressed through constraint metadata) to support choosing among the candidates. Once a choice is made, DAS will require the DAM WSDL (Web Service Description Language interface definition) to invoke DAM processing. Continuing the thought process also leads to the need for source metadata, with the combined results for this use case step being shown in Table 3-4. Note, the metadata, as notionally defined, supports the discovery and choice of DAM and corresponding data source before the source is ever accessed.

Table 3-4. Metadata types associated with Mediation/General Data Access use case

DAM metadata and notional elements
• DAM WSDL
• who responsible for WSDL (*person/organization metadata*)
• when it was last changed (*date metadata*)
• source from which DAM can retrieve data (pointer to *source metadata*)
• data that DAM can retrieve (including pointer to vocabulary description from which these data names are taken)
• assumptions/limitations that support deciding among DAMs (likely specified through *constraint metadata*)
source metadata and notional elements
• what source is (name and/or ID)
• who maintains it (*person/organization metadata*)
• *pedigree metadata* (describing previously evaluated data quality)
• index of DAM WSDLs (assuming more than one access is likely from a given source)

Systematic analysis of the use cases indicated in Table 3-3 resulted in many other types of metadata but also in a frequent duplication of metadata sets or the appearance of ones similar to previously identified sets. For example, one step from the ESM (Enterprise Service Management) use case states

> ISM (Integrated Service Management) correlates status data across CESs and provides resultant relevant operational status, performance, configuration, and security information to potential users.

and this implies the metadata types shown in Table 3-5.

Note, the analyses of the two examples result in the common appearance of date metadata and person/organization metadata. Such commonality is not unexpected because the underlying assumption for a metadata schema registry is that interoperability will be facilitated by reuse of common schema elements. However, the analysis highlights the granularity at which reuse is most likely to occur and the extent to which commonalities can be leveraged to further the goals and ultimate value of metadata creation, maintenance, and use.

Table 3-5. Metadata types associated with Enterprise Services Management use case

report metadata with notional elements
• who/what generated report (*person/organization metadata*)
• when generated (*date metadata*)
• link to directive requiring report
• type of report (linked to vocabulary of report types)
• subject of report (and link to vocabulary from which subject term derives, *e.g.* for ISM, if subset of management domain, link to definition of domain subsets)
• status of report (linked to vocabulary of report status)
• how/when report disseminated (possibly service link or *service metadata*)
• history (what did this supersede, what superseded this, when (actual or scheduled))

5.2 Second stage of analysis: forming conclusions across the use cases -- the modularization of metadata

The complete analysis of all the Table 3-3 use cases uncovered many commonalities and a factoring across the use cases indicated that metadata sets may be grouped into three categories based on their structure, their patterns of reuse, and the granularity of the concepts represented. The introduction of these categories is a fundamental difference in the way we look at metadata because instead of defining distinct, complex metadata structures for specific purposes, we introduce a modular approach of defining complex metadata in terms of more elementary metadata building blocks. This is consistent with the current paradigm for building software, but metadata has often been more compartmentalized, and this has hindered reuse in the same way as it hindered reuse in early software development. The DoD Metadata Registry similarly seeks to facilitate reuse, but metadata developers must search existing schemas and then extract useful parts. A more effective approach should be to define generic parts and support the developer in assembling the pieces.

As described in the following, the names chosen for the categories are *concepts*, *functions*, and *resources*. These names are less important than their use to convey the needs of metadata providers and consumers and the implications for a metadata system that will satisfy these needs. The immediate sections describe the characteristics of each category and the perspective implied by a modular approach. While references to the constituent metadata elements are introduced as needed to clarify the discussion of metadata categories, the detailed discussion of individual metadata sets is deferred until Section 5.3.

5.2.1   Concept metadata

Concept metadata is generally a set of information elements that convey a single elementary concept which is reused frequently as part of other metadata sets. The concept may require more than one element but it is likely to be a schema fragment (but still well-formed in the XML sense) rather than a complete schema. The following are a limited number of examples of concept metadata:

- name – the textual label by which an entity is identified, whether it be a physical object (such as a truck or a computer), a computational object (such as a schema, a data resource, or a service), or any other entity.
- person_name – possibly a special case of the general name; likely a collection of fragments representing formats for names of persons as these names are structured in different cultures, but with catalogued mappings between what are seen as common parts of the name variations
- datetime – formats representing date and time, likely built from the ISO date and time standard [7]
- pointer/reference/link – a standard means to point to other network accessible objects, most likely using the URI syntax for the target object
- keywords - textual terms defined within a referenced vocabulary (possibly defined by an XML namespace) that provides descriptive associations
- identifiers - unique means to identify an entity (possibly defined by an XML namespace), including a reference to documentation defining the identifier format and use.

Note that both the keywords and the identifiers include a reference to a defining vocabulary. The need to make such references a common part of the metadata space will be reiterated and expanded below.

The benefit of concept metadata is that it is focused and concise. If variations are required (see for example the HR-XML [8] work on a standard format for person names), it is far simpler to create a mapping (or indicate non-mapped elements) between variations of, say, a name type than it is to map schemas that are several (or dozens of) pages long. Reusing concise concept metadata and their associated mappings provide immediate interoperability over those elements even if there is not total understanding of a complex schema that incorporates the concept metadata.

5.2.2   Functions metadata

A review of the AoA use cases shows a strong dependence on processes and the recurring need to identify mechanisms and constraints that enable use of an entity in a manner consistent with needs and requirements of both users and resources. Function metadata combines concept metadata sets, simpler function metadata sets, and additional unique metadata to capture descriptive and access information needed to support such reusable functions. For example, access/invocation metadata collects information to support data access or service invocation; pedigree metadata describes pedigrees that have been established for various resources. The functions themselves may be fairly elementary, such as the person/organization metadata, or a more complex combination of concept metadata and more elementary function metadata, such as the access/invocation and pedigree examples. The following are a number of frequently occurring function metadata sets and a brief description of the function each provides:

- Person/Organization – identity and contact information for a person or organization (using concept metadata such as name, address, email)
- Title/Position - identity and contact information based on specific role (*e.g.* Director of IT) rather than current person in the role; may redirect to instance of Person/Organization metadata
- Creation/Modification - critical information about latest change to an identified resource; information would include contact information (using Person/Organization or Title/Position metadata) of who made change, datetime (concept) metadata of when change was made
- Access/Invocation - means to access a service or other resource; includes the WSDL interface, constraints and policies for access, and assumptions/constraints associated with the processing that will be performed or data that will be provided; references identified using pointer/reference/link (concept) metadata
- Constraint – means to identify rules that define constraints, limitations, and assumptions related to any entity; includes party responsible for definition and maintenance, means to access, and recommended associated processing of; references identified using pointer/reference/link (concept) metadata
- Pedigree documented level of "goodness" as qualified by vocabulary through which pedigree level is defined, associated constraint set with details of pedigree criteria, means of evaluating entity against criteria; references identified using pointer/reference/link (concept) metadata
- Log - means to identify (including responsible party) and describe access to logs for tracking use and modification of a resource; assume logs maintained external from but linked to the entity being tracked

Section 5.3 contains a detailed description and identifies notional elements for many function metadata sets. The notional element list for each set can be considered a baseline but the expressivity of the baseline can be easily expanded by adding other concept or function metadata. By considering existing metadata sets as building blocks, a scalable mechanism is defined to incorporate previously defined semantics. With current schemas, some of the constituent elements are optional when a metadata producer creates metadata instances; for modular metadata, the inclusion of additional concept or function metadata is the optional extensibility mechanism. By reusing building blocks, a metadata producer can exercise the established context to fully describe the entity at hand.

The modular construction is important for immediate interoperability and can provide enhanced capability as the quality, completeness, and sophistication of the metadata increases. For example, consider having the metadata sets expressed as ontologies, where these ontologies would capture not only the class-subclass structure but also the axioms relating the classes. Then, if we capture mappings between variations of a metadata type (such as mentioned above for the name concept) as additional axioms, these axioms can be combined and processed by available inference engines to establish broader understanding. Adding a new variation would not require mapping to every existing one because existing relationships would be leveraged to establish the meaning of the new variation within the existing context.

5.2.3   Resource metadata

While concept metadata describes elementary concepts and function metadata describes the information related to common activities, resource metadata combines these to describe the assets that can be utilized to respond to user needs. Unlike concepts and functions, the types of resources tend to be more coarsely defined and more limited in number. An SOA environment has data and processing resources, and to these a GES discussion adds others, specifically entities requiring content metadata and structural metadata. The description and relation between these resources are the focus of this section.

A *data resource* is a source of content. It accepts a request and returns a value or set of values in response. The return can be an entity (such as a particular schema), an attribute of an entity (such as when the schema was last modified), or any numerical or textual value or set of values. The content can be static objects stored in some repository or dynamically generated through the use of a processing resource. Data about a missile that is stored in a database is content. The weather forecast for tomorrow in Iraq is content generated from a weather simulation. In a net-centric environment, the requester does not know the format from which the response is retrieved or how it is generated.

A *processing resource* is one that accepts a task and returns a status indicating the extent to which the task was completed and information on how the state of entities changed as a result of the processing. One or more processing resources may be invoked as part of a process of submitting a query and being returned a response. From the standpoint of a user (either human or machine), it is unimportant what combination of data and processing resources are invoked as long as the request is satisfied.

Content metadata as described for DDMS comprises metadata to "aid in precision discovery" and includes such specialized metadata as that describing geospatial coverage. While such a description is consistent with the findings of the AoA analysis, a broader description may be more useful. Table 3-6 shows a comparison of the notional metadata elements for content, data, and service (*i.e.*, a processing resource) metadata. (The rows are solely for convenience in comparing like elements.) The interesting point is that the notional elements for content and data resource metadata were collected at separate times (during the overall analysis) but give very similar results. During the analysis, a data resource was considered the asset from which information is retrieved while content was thought of as the retrieved information. This leads to minor differences in the metadata elements, such as content metadata includes the creation/modification function metadata while the data resource metadata assumes there may be an update policy to be referenced. However, one element of the "update cycle" is "last update", a direct parallel to and possible use of creation/modification function metadata. Furthermore, while not explicitly noted, version and status metadata for services implicitly include creation/modification information on when and by whom the version or status was assigned. The conclusion is that while content metadata may be a useful grouping, it is not important whether we classify the metadata associated with an entity as data resource metadata or content metadata as long as the component metadata makes use of and references the same common building blocks. As with update cycle *vs.* creation/modification, it is not the *a priori* classification that is important but rather providing the metadata that is most appropriate in facilitating eventual use of the entity.

Table 3-6. Comparison of notional elements for content, data resource, and service metadata

Content	Data Resource	Service
- name of content - description (text) - formal descriptors/keywords indicating function - pointer/link to vocabulary defining descriptors/keywords	- name - description (text) - formal descriptors/keywords indicating function - pointer/link to vocabulary defining descriptors/keywords	- name - description (text) - formal descriptors/keywords indicating function - pointer/link to vocabulary defining descriptors/keywords
- pointer to content (where content exists/is stored)	- unique identifier (could be URI)	- unique identifier (could be URI)
- creation/modification metadata	- update cycle -- description of update policy -- refresh cycle (may be "continuous") -- last update	- version (format for defining insignificant, minor, major changes) - status (*e.g.* current version, beta test, superseded; status definitions to be referenced)
- type of content (log, data, processing, ...) - format (MIME type)		
- responsible party -- type (Person/Org, Title/Position, ...) -- Person/Organization metadata <or> Reference by title/position metadata	- responsible party -- type (Person/Org, Title/Position, ...) -- Person/Organization metadata <or> Reference by title/position metadata	- responsible party for service maintenance -- type (Person/Org, Title/Position, ...) -- Person/Organization metadata <or> Reference by title/position metadata - responsible party for service operation -- (same as service maintenance)
- access/invocation metadata sets	- Access/invocation metadata - prequalified list (individuals, organizations (individual who have association with), roles) of who can invoke	- Access/invocation metadata - prequalified list (individuals, organizations (individual who have association with), roles) of who can invoke - Service Level Agreement metadata
- Constraints/assumptions metadata - pedigree metadata sets	- Constraints/assumptions metadata - pedigree metadata sets	- Constraints/assumptions metadata - pedigree metadata sets
- Security metadata (including access privileges required)	- Security metadata (including access privileges required)	- Security metadata (including access privileges required)

Structural metadata can be considered a subset of data resources (or alternately, content) but it has typically been given more prominence because it is seen as the prerequisite resource in the build *vs.* runtime perspective for developing and using metadata systems. For example, the DoD Metadata Registry Guide [9] describes Information Resources, Data Assets, and Data Services, where Information Resources refer to XML schema, XML style-sheets, document type definitions, attributes, data structures and other types of structural metadata. From the AoA analysis, specific metadata types that could be considered structural metadata include metadata for schemas, message holders, message objects, and possibly other network and device descriptions. However, several conclusions emerge from the AoA analysis that suggest a less prominent role for structural metadata as a special category. In an SOA environment, integration is done through service interfaces rather than the traditional wiring together of components. Thus, the need for detailed format information is encapsulated in the creation of the service interface, a task generally performed by those already knowing the format details. Secondly, the discussion of schema metadata in Section 5.3 suggests that the build time *vs.* runtime distinction may not be as useful as a query *vs.* populate paradigm. The AoA analysis identifies analogous metadata functions across build and runtime activities, and a query *vs.* populate perspective emphasizes how common tools and techniques are more natural if structural components are considered as another resource with metadata similar to that shown in Table 3-6. Following this perspective, supporting metadata, such as statistics on where a schema is used or by whom, is equally relevant to nonstructural entities, and effective reuse would be facilitated by having such common functions available as part of any metadata and supported by metadata registries.

5.3   Discussion of select metadata sets – paradigms for using modular metadata

The previous section emphasized the modular definition of metadata sets, introduced the concept, function, and resource metadata categories, and provided some detail on specific metadata sets in each category. Recall that the metadata sets are the result of first identifying metadata types and constituent elements that were implied by AoA use cases and then collecting similar metadata sets across use cases. The result is a collection corresponding to the three metadata categories, with the associated metadata sets described through their notional metadata elements and the conclusions that emerge from considering the functions that the metadata must support. There was no concerted effort to make the constituent elements completely consistent across all metadata sets because different functions were suggested by different use cases and one of the perceived benefits of a modular structure is that, once defined, different elements can be used where deemed necessary by a metadata developer. Thus at this stage, it is more important to introduce a range of ideas than to definitively attach any given idea to a specific metadata set. The remainder of this section describes details of several metadata sets that are expected to have high reuse. In addition, the descriptions provide a context for suggesting additional functionality and useful perspectives that may be enable the broad range of GES expectations.

Access/Invocation metadata

The Access/Invocation metadata set is a prominent example because, in a SOA, the details of access of any information resource or invoking any processing resource should be hidden from the user. This is most commonly seen as the function of the resource's WSDL. However, access in a composable environment requires more than just the details of the interface; it includes the information a user needs to decide if the resource is appropriate for an intended use. Thus, the Access/Invocation metadata should include items such as

- a description of the interface corresponding to this metadata
- the type of access (read, write, delete) supported
- WSDL description
- who is responsible for the interface
- when and by whom the interface was last changed
- details on constraints (including security and intellectual property rights), assumptions, and pedigree
- details on service level agreements (SLAs)
- what permissions are necessary to use the interface
- who is prequalified to use the interface
- who has certified the interface for use

The prequalified list is a notional mechanism by which users who have met all necessary criteria can be granted expedited access. Possibly, this could be done by a service that checks whether the criteria (*e.g.*, policies, terms of use, access category definitions) identified as part of this metadata set has been satisfied and registers with the criteria to be informed of changes that might affect continued prequalification status. The prequalification service would maintain a list of the entities it has qualified and revalidate the applicable members of the list if a criteria changes.

The certified list is similar but in this case a Community of Interest (COI) could certify a resource as having an authoritative status (per its documented definition of authoritative) or be preferred for use. The resource would note who has certified it (a possible factor in whether someone outside the certifying organization wanted to use it) and the COI would maintain a list of its pre-certified resources. The certification process could also be done through a service that ensured the certification lists for resources and the COI remain consistent.

Constraint and Pedigree metadata sets

In a SOA environment, constraints will describe a host of assumptions, restrictions, and conditions related to a resource, not only to determine whether a prospective user should be permitted access but for the prospective user to decide whether the resource is appropriate for the immediate tasking needs. Notional elements include:

- name and description of the constraint set,
- version number and link to the definition of the version terminology,
- Access/Invocation metadata for reading the constraint set,
- Access/Invocation metadata for the preferred processing agent for evaluating an entity against the referenced constraint set
- pointer/link to entities that are evaluated against this constraint set.

Constraint definitions are a precursor to establishing pedigrees. Pedigree metadata is most often thought of as that information that would be useful in evaluating the pedigree of an entity. On further analysis, it becomes clear that such supporting information, rather than being separately identified as pedigree metadata, is interspersed throughout other metadata sets, such as the responsible party for a service access or the date a resource was created or modified. Moreover, the vital metadata is less what goes into evaluating a pedigree and more which pedigrees have been satisfied and how has that been determined. This leads to the following notional elements:

- the pedigree which describes the status of the resource,
- a pointer/link to the constraint set which specifies the conditions satisfied or not satisfied by an entity with this pedigree,
- a pointer/link to the processing engine used to evaluate the constraint set and establish the pedigree,
- when the pedigree was established,
- if applicable, when the pedigree expires.

An entity can have multiple pedigrees corresponding to different constraint sets or different degrees of satisfying a constraint set. A pedigree may be as straightforward as to say a metadata instance has been validated against a schema or it may capture a partial validation which in and of itself has merit.

Aspects of pedigree are similar to prequalification described as part of Access/Invocation metadata. Establishing pedigree could be done through a separate service that performs certification by evaluating the entity with respect to an identified constraint set and then appending the pedigree metadata set to the entity's existing metadata. Thus, an entity's metadata would not just be a static set submitted by someone during a registration process but could also be modified by authorized parties during the life cycle of the metadata. The pedigree evaluation engine would not only write to the entity's metadata but would also register with the constraint set and the evaluating engine so the pedigree could be revalidated should the constraint or the evaluation mechanism change.

Schema metadata

Schemas serve in several distinct roles to enable metadata functions that are an integral part in the typical build time and runtime scenarios. In particular, for *querying metadata*, schema elements provide the available search parameters for the query submitter. Someone querying to identify an entity supplies target values for some subset of the schema elements for metadata describing the entity, and the query results indicate those instances whose metadata values best match/approximate the target values. The query process is the same for all queries but uses different schemas as the basis for queries of different entities. For *populating metadata*, schema elements provide the descriptive parameters for which a metadata producer provides descriptive values. The populating process is the same for populating any metadata instance, again using the schema appropriate to the entity at hand.

During the traditional build time, a schema developer will search metadata describing existing schemas to find one(s) to reuse as the basis for a new schema. If we assume there is descriptive information about schemas and the query provides more than a string match to schema elements, then the metadata template for both the query to find the existing schemas and the template to populate to describe the eventual new schema is a schema-for-schemas[3].

During the runtime activity of a metadata producer needing to create metadata for some new entity, the producer will search metadata describing existing schemas to find one to use as the template for a new metadata instance. The metadata template for the query is the schema-for-schemas and the metadata template to populate to describe the new entity is the schema identified by the query.

---

[3]   One class of resources requiring descriptive metadata are the schemas that serve as the structure for metadata instances. Thus, there is a schema for describing schemas that is likely produced by those organizing and maintaining a metadata registry. This schema-for-schemas follows all the rules for schemas and its metadata description is an instance of itself. While this logic appears circular, it is consistent with descriptions in the XML Schema specification. The power of this construction is that the metadata for describing schemas is no different from the metadata describing any other class of entities, and thus the metadata can be created, organized, and searched by common mechanisms.

For a metadata consumer needing to find an entity to support a runtime need, there is an initial query or browse phase to identify a schema that describes the required entity (in the other scenarios just described, the required entity is a schema and the corresponding schema is the schema-for-schemas). Using the schema found from the initial search/browse, the consumer will search metadata instances describing the required entity to find one to satisfy the current runtime need. The metadata template for this query is the one from the initial search/browse and there is no populate metadata phase.

Note that the above scenarios for the three user types follow similar processes. When one is looking for an entity to meet their needs, they assume the role of someone querying to identify resources. This could be a schema developer looking for schema fragments upon which to build, a metadata producer looking for a schema to populate to describe their current resource, or a metadata consumer looking for some entity relevant to a COI task. When one needs to create metadata instances, those instances are created by providing values to the elements of the relevant schema. For the schema developer, the organizing schema is the schema-for-schemas and the metadata produced is that describing new schemas. For the producer of metadata for resources other than schemas, the organizing schema is any of the other schemas developed by schema developers. The process of creating metadata for schemas or metadata for any other entities is the same.

A conclusion of the analysis is that a major distinction in the scenarios is not build *vs.* run time but query (including use of query results) *vs.* populate. To support this, the notional elements for schema metadata could include:

- schema name
- schema description
- schema keywords and link to keyword vocabulary definition
- who created schema and when created
- how to access (e.g. WSDL, if through service)
- which schemas incorporate this schema (*i.e.*, use as a building block)
- which schemas are incorporated in this schema (*i.e.*, used as building blocks)
- how many instances use this schema
- list of entity owners with largest number of instances using this schema
- list of domains which recommend using this schema

Note the last five elements provide information to describe a context for this schema and facilitate reuse. The statistics are likely collected by the metadata registry and their values would be maintained by the registry or delivered through a registry service. The specifics of those metadata elements and their eventual use should be the subject of further design.

Log metadata

Especially as relates to security, there is considerable discussion of NCES or any service framework being able to trace and audit transactions. In addition, in a composable environment, it is not enough for a user to submit a request and get back an answer if the answer does not include information specifying how the answer was generated and from where input data was obtained. This is important not only for immediate documentation but also for repeatability and efficiency in executing later requests. For example, if a user submits the exact same request on two consecutive shifts and is returned different responses, the user must know whether the difference is due to a change in the input data or a change in the processing or data resource. In addition, considerable compute and communications resources could be used in determining how to satisfy a complex request, and it is advisable to be able to repeat a previous established process rather than reinventing it for every request.

Log metadata assumes that the processing steps and utilized resources are captured through an auditing process and the resultant log will be stored and catalogued for future reference and use. The notional elements chosen to support such activity include:

- link to the log
- link to the entity for which the log applies
- type of log (*e.g.*, access, update, processing steps)
- access/invocation for reading log
- access/invocation for executing log

Note, one access/invocation element is defined for reading the log contents, and the other, assuming the log exists in a form that can be considered an executable resource, defines the invocation of that resource.

6.   CONSOLIDATED VIEW OF METADATA CLASSES

The discussion in Section 4 detailed goals that metadata is meant to empower and the metadata groupings that have been derived to enable realization of those goals. Although the authors of each effort were familiar with the preceding results, the various groupings were conceived somewhat independently, taking a different perspective on framing the problem. This should not be thought of as duplicated effort because the critical role assigned to metadata in a service-oriented architecture has many facets which have only just begun to get attention both with respect to NCES and in the general Web community. Indeed, the different perspective have helped to build a more complete metadata picture. The focus of this section is to begin to assemble that larger picture.

The Net-Centric Data Strategy defines seven DoD data goals and these can be considered the benchmarks by which any metadata strategy would be measured. In discussing approaches to achieving these goals, the Data Strategy introduces high level metadata types and functions, and this provides an initial set of metadata categories. DDMS focuses primarily on one of the net-centric goals, Discovery, and begins building the metadata tagging framework to capture information by which existing communities discriminate among entities that can satisfy their user needs. The AoA analysis derives metadata specifics from the more general perspective of use cases covering a number of NCES core services, including Discovery. For the AoA analysis, the focus is on enabling functionality implied by each step of the use cases and this often requires simultaneously satisfying several of the Data Strategy goals.

The different perspectives lead to identifying different metadata categories and specifying different levels of detail. With the broader perspective, the AoA analysis generated less specificity at the element level than that provided by the DDMS focus on Discovery. However, there is significant commonality at the basic concepts level, such as name, description, or contact information, and in most cases, a more complete solution is a combination of the two sets of results. For example, DDMS dedicated significant effort in specifying security details while such details are lacking from the AoA analysis. Security is of vital importance to NCES and all Web services but the AoA analysis time frame did not afford the opportunity to fully analyze security concerns for which DDMS provides guidance.

While there is significant agreement among the identified metadata categories, there are also some differences in structure and content. With respect to structure, the AoA analysis found significant benefit in a modular framework where small schema fragments were readily reused in building more complex but also reusable structures. For example, the DDMS Resource Set specifies metadata structures for the roles of Creator, Publisher, and Contributor. There are identical elements within each of these structures but the most visible equivalence is implied by nomenclature and any formal relationship is embedded in the DDMS schema. Using more transparent metadata building blocks, such as Person/Organization, would support a common structure defining many roles, possibly with a metadata element being added to identify the role itself. This also highlights the importance of identifying the vocabulary from which the roles or other terms are defined. By making a vocabulary identifier an integral part of the metadata structure, the framework is more extensible, reusable, and interoperable in the future because new roles can be added at the instance level rather than having to add to and modify the schema structure itself. DDMS has several metadata constructs where the Qualifier tag is used to identify vocabulary, but there may be significant benefit to making this a standard part of the infrastructure.

With respect to metadata content, one area where there is a difference is in the perceived need for Format metadata. Format details are critical in a traditional integration because this is the level at which developers needed to wire together the often diverse components from which their standalone systems would take form. Consistent with this approach, DDMS highlights Format as one of the core layer categories. However, the emphasis of a SOA is on the Web service interface, reducing the need for format detail because this is hidden by the standard definition of the service interface. Thus, the format detail is now limited to service developers who are likely part of the project teams responsible for the resource being exposed by the service. The format detail would be available internally to the team and will be of less interest to most of the community who directly or indirectly uses metadata to enable other service capabilities.

While interest in format details may be reduced, the composable aspects of a SOA environment elevates the need for resource pedigree, both in terms of the information needed to establish pedigree and the means and results of evaluating this information. DDMS follows a more traditional approach by identifying information likely to be useful in evaluating pedigree and collecting these in the Resource Set elements. The AoA analysis found that the relevant information is naturally distributed across a number of metadata categories and there was limited value in collecting these under one structure. This is because most information will have multiple uses and higher quality metadata is likely to result by allowing the metadata provider to use (and reference) a local vocabulary rather than extract information to an imposed structure. In addition, the information useful in establishing pedigree is likely to expand and evolve over time, resulting in use of information that had not been previously associated with pedigree. Moreover, the importance lies not in collecting the possible information bits required as input but in documenting how pedigree has been evaluated, what context defines the criteria, and what is the result of the evaluation. Thus, the emphasis shifts to metadata that describes the rules and constraint sets which define any particular pedigree and identifying the processing resources used to evaluate entities against these rules. Pedigree and also logging are examples of functions with greater importance in a SOA environment, and these merit in-depth consideration in the future.

Finally, there are several considerations that apply across all the efforts to describe and categorize metadata. First, the semantics of the metadata tags must be clear and unambiguous. In general, this is done but the Qualifier tag in DDMS is one example where a tag is overloaded and its meaning can be very different depending on context. If there are basic information items that are specific to only a few metadata contexts, these should be defined in terms of metadata building blocks and then consistently reused across all relevant metadata sets. Flexibility in assigning names and terms can be accommodated by emphasizing separate, either NCES or COI defined, vocabularies from which terms can be referenced. This again provides flexibility at the operational level without requiring changes to the infrastructure to accommodate changes in the mission. XML Namespaces are a valuable example in providing a degree of clarity and flexibility. The namespace identifies a unique vocabulary but does not specify the descriptive resources at the indicated URI. Thus, the resources retrieved by dereferencing the URI can be tailored to the entities being described. Defining what resources support the user needs and NCES mission may be a useful area of further investigation.

A final consideration is life cycle issues. The emphasis up to now has been on encouraging metadata production by the resource owners, and while the metadata is not necessarily static over time, the assumption was that changes in the metadata would remain the responsibility of the owners. The AoA analysis uncovered several scenarios where metadata may be modified and augmented over the resource life cycle and these changes will be made by authorized entities other than the resource owner. For example, if one organization has established a pedigree for a resource, this may be vital information for another organization considering the same resource. The pedigree is not under the control of the resource owner and the owner should not be involved in augmenting the metadata to reflect the someone else's pedigree. Distributed, authorized modifications and additions to metadata have not been adequately considered in the past and may be a vital capability in the future.

7.   CONCLUSIONS

Metadata is an important enabler for any service-oriented architecture, and is especially critical in support of GIG Enterprise Services and the Net-Centric Data Strategy goals. The discussion compared several efforts to describe metadata and introduced the benefits of a modular approach to metadata structure. It also highlighted supporting capabilities that could be implemented through metadata registries. These capabilities include
- providing a standard way to link any term to a defining vocabulary
- providing services to augment metadata in a consistent manner and as required to introduce or update descriptive information that is outside the

control of the associated resource, *e.g.* to track certified and prequalified use of resources

- collecting and making available statistics that describe the use and reuse of schemas and other resources.

The discussion is not meant as a definitive specification of particular metadata types or sets, but to provide insight into the requirements for creating, maintaining, and using metadata in a SOA environment. The reference to NCES Analysis of Alternative use cases demonstrates the aspects of metadata that directly impact the GIG ES and accomplishing the Net-Centric Data Strategy goals.

REFERENCES

[1] ASD(NII) CIO Global Information Grid Core Enterprise Services Strategy, Draft version 1.1a, 9 July, 2003, http://www.defenselink.mil/nii/org/cio/doc/ GIG_ES_Core_Enterprise_Services_Strategy_V1-1a.pdf

[2] DoD CIO Memorandum, DoD Net-Centric Data Strategy, Version 1.0, 9 May 2003, http://www.defenselink.mil/nii/org/cio/doc/Net-Centric-Data-Strategy-2003-05-092.pdf

[3] Web Services Description Language (WSDL): version 1.1, http://www.w3.org/TR/wsdl; version 2.0, http://www.w3.org/2002/ws/desc/ .

[4] DoD Discovery Metadata Specification (DDMS), Version 1.0, 29 September 2003, DASD (Deputy CIO), http://diides.ncr.disa.mil/mdreg/user/DDMS.cfm.

[5] Net-Centric Enterprise Services (NCES) Analysis of Alternatives (AoA) Report, 4 May 2004.

[6] DISA Concept of Operations for DoD Metadata, draft, September 2004.

[7] Data elements and interchange formats - Information interchange - Representation of dates and times, ISO 8601 : 2000.

[8] HR-XML Consortium, *Person Name 1.2 Recommendation*, 26 February 2003.

[9] DoD Metadata Registry Guide, draft for public comment, http://diides.ncr.disa.mil/mdregHomePage/mdregHome.portal

Chapter 4

DISTRIBUTED GEOSPATIAL INTELLIGENCE INTEGRATION AND INTEROPERABILITY THROUGH THE GIDB® PORTAL SYSTEM

John T. Sample and Frank P. McCreedy
Naval Research Laboratory, Stennis Space Center, MS 39529, USA;

Abstract: This chapter will present the potential benefits from integrated and interoperable geographic data sources. It will discuss the challenges and options involved in creating a geographic portal system and will use the Naval Research Laboratory's Geospatial Information Database (GIDB®) as an example system. The GIDB is the leading tool for integration of geospatial intelligence for homeland security applications. It currently integrates over 600 sources of geospatial intelligence and provides them to users worldwide.

Keywords: Horizontal Integration, Data Fusion, GIS, XML

1. INTRODUCTION

Recent developments in computer networking, data management and web services have resulted in a surge in the amount of geographic data available on the internet. The data can include road maps, weather forecasts, and locations of hospitals. Federal, state and local governments as well as private organizations have begun to make their geographic databases available to the public on the internet. Among these collections, nationwide road networks and aerial imagery are included. Furthermore, one can find locations of military bases, nuclear power plants, and governmental buildings by simple internet searches. Local governments provide locations of fire hydrants, mail routes and voting precincts on their data servers. Given the vast amount of data available on the internet, the opportunity arises to make effective use of all these sources. The driving concept behind the Naval Research Laboratory's Geospatial Information Database (GIDB®) is to link together as many of these distributed sources as possible and creates a portal that makes all these sources work together and appear as a single source of data.

The GIDB Portal System is currently used by the U.S. National Guard Bureau-Counter Drug (NGB-CD) within their Digital Mapping System (DMS). The DMS is based almost entirely upon the GIDB Portal System. It's thin, thick and PDA clients are based on the GIDB client packages. The portal software and server directory is the same as the GIDB's. The purpose of the DMS is to provide maps in an easy to use format to thousands of law enforcement personnel. Because the GIDB is a totally license free package, the system can be transitioned to all of these users at very little incremental cost.

The DMS is a key technology for National Guard Bureau Counter-Drug Activities. It helps officers locate drug activity, monitor borders and provide event security. The DMS is currently utilized by several thousand registered federal, state and local law enforcement personel, as well as, other first responders and support staff.

1.1   Data Interoperability Possibilities

There are many reasons to try to integrate numerous data sources. First, there is the potential for synergy. In other words, geographical data types can become more useful when combined with other types. Examples of this include, combining a weather map with a road map to plan routes that avoid storms or combining aerial imagery with previous locations of marijuana growth sites to plan drug control flights. Another reason to link together data sources in a dynamic way is because the amount of data available is too great to store and maintain in one place. A collection of integrated and distributed data sources can "divide and conquer" the problem of managing vast geographic data collections.

Figure 1 shows aerial imagery from the USGS enhanced with a road map the U.S. Census Bureau.

Figure 4-1. Aerial Imagery Enhanced with Road Map

The image in Figure 2 shows a map of Seattle, WA. The image was taken from a map created by the GIDB in its participation in a U.S. Department of Homeland Security exercise. It displays locations of simulated terrorist attacks alongside the model of a plume from a "dirty bomb." The plume is shown spreading westward from Seattle.

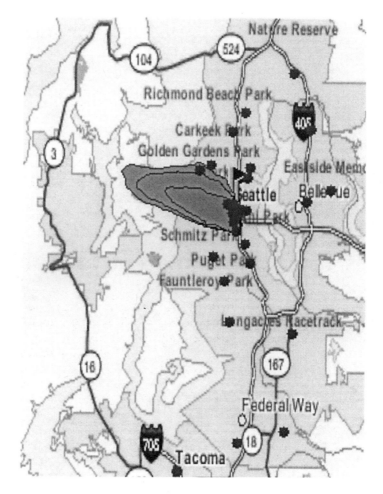

Figure 4-2. Map of Seattle with Simulated Plume Model

Figures 1 and 2 are examples of the possible products possible with more complete integration of geographic data sources. Another advantage is data redundancy, with a network of integrated data servers; we can collect data sets from multiple sources. Thus, we are not dependant on any single server.

1.2   Data Interoperability Challenges

Linking together all these data sources is not necessarily a straightforward task. There are many technical as well as conceptual issues to be resolved. First, geographical data on the internet exists in a variety of formats, including various types of imagery and vector (geometric) data types. Also, the data is available through numerous proprietary or open communication protocols which must be negotiated independently. Finally, data sources are to some extent transient. They have intermittent availability and their data sets change over time. These issues have conceptually straightforward solutions, but much effort and expertise is required for practical implementation.

Also, what is the best way to present all of this data? Should we simply heap it all together into one large mass of data? Or should we sort and arrange the sources, thus controlling access to the sources? This set of issues is not easily resolved, because different users have different needs. Some users will want a canned presentation; others will want a lower level of access to the data. Also, how should users be allowed to interact with the data sources? Should their queries be passed through an intermediate broker or sent directly to the source of data? This chapter will present solutions to these issues and other challenges solved by the GIDB Portal System.

1.3   Traditional and Net-Centric Approaches

Any solution to the problem of distributed geographic data integration will almost be "net-centric" by default. The concept of a geospatial data portal is dependent upon widespread and reliable network usage. However, there are specific requirements that must be met for a software solution to be considered "net-centric." These requirements are defined in the "DoD Net-Centric Data Strategy."[1] This is the official policy of the United States Department of Defense and provides general guidance towards more effective use of information/data resources.

"Net-centricity is the realization of a networked environment, including infrastructure, systems, processes, and people, that enables a completely different approach to warfighting and business operations."[1] The goal of net-centric information management is to make data visible, available and useable to any authorized users on the network. This is a significant departure from previous and current data management practices.

Many current data management practices are classically "stove-piped," that is, data is managed along rigid point-to-point paths. Consider this example: a system for determining the depth of the ocean in key areas is constructed. The components are (1) a sonar array for collecting soundings, (2) a software package for producing a grid of the data, (3) a software package that applies tide corrections to the grid, and (4) a software package for storage and display of the data. In this system, the sonar array produces soundings data in a custom proprietary format designed by the sonar maker.

The software that produces the grids is programmed to read in the custom soundings format and output a grid in another custom format. Likewise the remaining software components are each specially configured to input and output customized data products for this specific process. Figure 3 is a diagram of this example system.

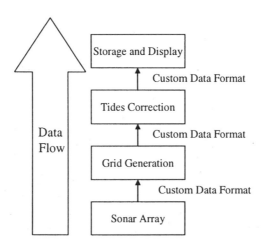

Figure 4-3. Example Stove Piped System

This system has numerous weaknesses. First, the system has significant configuration management requirements. Each component of the system is dependent upon all the others. If the sonar array software is upgraded and produces soundings in a slightly different format, the gridding software has to be changed to accept the new soundings format. Likewise, if the gridding software is changed to produce higher resolution grids, then the tides correction software has to be changed to accept the higher resolution grids. The end result is a never ending cycle of system changes that puts the system into a constant "debugging" state. Many useful software systems have been doomed to failure in this manner.

Another significant weakness of this system is its built-in rigidity. Consider a joint operation between multiple nations, in which each nation has its own system for computing bathymetry in given areas. Each system has its own versions of the earlier listed components. However, since each system has its own custom data formats, the components cannot interact with each other. Figure 4 shows three example systems, each operating independently of the others.

If one wanted to apply the tide correction from System 1 to the data collected by System 2, they would have to alter the software to accept additional data formats. This is hardly practical in an operational environment, but it is the type of situation often faced. A better solution is that described in Figure 5. In this example, each stage of processing produces a standardized format for data that can be shared by multiple systems.

There are numerous standards producing organizations as well as de facto standards for geographical data formats. A higher initial investment is often required to implement standardized data formats within a system, but the long term benefits are numerous. In this chapter we will discuss how standard data formats and access protocols can positively impact a data management strategy.

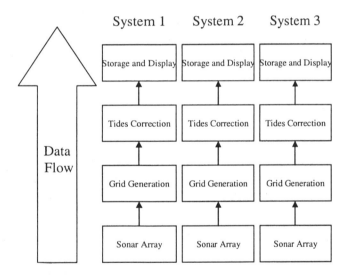

Figure 4-4. Example of Three Stove Piped Systems

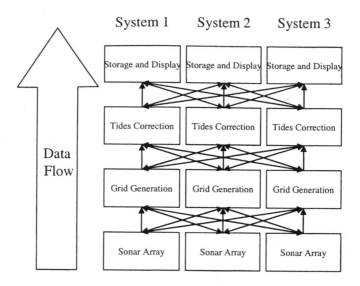

Figure 4-5. Improved System Configuration

2.   SOURCES OF GEOGRAPHIC DATA

The impact of a portal of integrated geographical data sources is dependent upon its constituent data sources. This section presents a survey of the sources of geographic data on the internet, describes the data types available and outlines the communication protocols used to access the data.

2.1   Types of Geographic Data

In general terms there are two main types of geographic data, vector and raster. Vector geographic features use geometric primitives such as points, lines, curves, and polygons to represent map features such as roads, rivers, nations. Raster geographic data types are generally structures that consist of rectangular arrays of pixels or points with given values. This can include scanned maps and charts, airborne, satellite, and sonar imagery. Additional data types include three-dimensional data products, like bathymetry and terrain models, and multi-media data types, like video and audio recordings.

Figure 4-6. Vector Data: North American Boundaries

Figure 6 shows a vector representation of the boundaries of North American countries. Figure 7 shows a raster map based on satellite images of North America.

Figure 4-7. Raster Data: Satellite Based Image of North America

2.2   Types of Geographic Data Servers

Geographic data servers can be quite varied. Some are built on robust database management systems (DBMS). Others are simply transport mechanisms for sensor data or other observations. The most basic types of geographic data servers can be as simple as a web page or FTP (File Transport Protocol) site with geographic data files available.

2.2.1   File Based Servers

This category of servers is simple, but an important source of data. For example, public and private weather services provide imagery and forecasts on the websites in the form of pre-rendered maps. These maps are available as web pages, and can be accessed through simple hypertext transport protocol (HTTP) requests. Other examples are the United States Geological Survey (USGS) and the United States Department of Transportation, each of whom have large datasets of public geographic data available for download from their websites.

These data sources often change with time, and thus have to be monitored continuously. Also, they offer data in multiple formats which have to be independently interpreted. These sites are simple to use one at a time, but collecting data from hundreds of these sites on a daily basis is beyond the scope of any single user.

2.2.2   GIS Based Servers

The next broad category of geographic servers consists of more comprehensive software systems that can provide a user with a complete, though often specialized, map view. These are usually expensive and advanced server systems, which include a DBMS, fully functional geographic information system (GIS), and some type of map renderer. Most of these systems require users to use a specific client software package to access the server. Several vendors currently provide these types of software; examples are ESRI's ArcIMS and AutoDesk's MapGuide.

These systems provide query functionality for a variety of fields including area-of-interest, time and theme. They display data in different layers on a interactive map view. While very powerful, they are almost always restricted to accessing data that resides under the control of the server. Thus, the system is responsible for data maintenance, backups, updates, etc.

These are the most common forms of geographical data server used in geographic data portals. They are well suited to this type of integration, because they do much of the computational "heavy lifting" and produce complete or nearly complete maps that are ready for viewing.

Interfaces to these types of servers vary and can be troublesome to integrate. They involve a mixture of open and closed proprietary protocols. Most servers offer some type of programmatic interface so that the data can be queried and retrieved. However, some restrict usage to their own client software packages.

These servers are often maintained by federal, state or local governments and contain data relevant to the respective missions of the owning organization. For example, the United States Department of Agriculture maintains a large collection of data on plant and animal life in the U.S. on a geographic data server.

2.2.3 Specialty Servers

In addition to the previously mentioned servers, there exists a class of geographic data servers that have been constructed to suit specialized purposes. These purposes include distributing oceanographic and atmospheric forecasts, satellite imagery, locations of smallpox vaccine reserves, and other specialized products. This class of server varies greatly in the type and amount of data they offer, but they share a common characteristic: they almost always employ a custom interface for queries and data access. These custom protocols were designed to suit the needs of the specialty server and little more, and to integrate these servers into a coherent data source, one has to implement each protocol on its own.

3. WEB SERVICES

"The World Wide Web is more and more used for application to application communication. The programmatic interfaces made available are referred to as *Web services*."[2]

"Web services provide a standard means of interoperating between different software applications, running on a variety of platforms and/or frameworks."[3]

Space here is not permitted to fully explain the importance and potential impact of web services on the data integration problem. However, a brief discussion is essential to understand the future of geographical data integration. As the above quotes indicate, Web services are about application to application communication i.e. consistent, standardized programmatic interfaces that allow complex software systems to interoperate often in an automatic fashion.

Two key factors are important prerequisites before Web services can be implemented in an effective manner. They are: (1) a pool of software tools to publish and maintain various software services and (2) domain specific standards for sharing information between platforms. The pool of software tools has become somewhat rich in recent years, mostly due to the contributions of the open source community with support from the software industry.

Within the geographic data domain, several new standards have come forward to facilitate data integration and interoperability. The OpenGIS Consortium (OGC) has proposed a number of standards for communicating geographic data and metadata. These standards are available from http://www.opengis.org. Table 1 lists and describes the most significant OGC standards.

4.   DEFINING A GEOGRAPHIC DATA PORTAL

In the previous sections we have described types of distributed geographic data sources and methods to access them. However, what should a portal look like that brings them all together and creates a single source for all these data types? In this section, we will examine several different types of geographic portals that are currently used and discuss the relative benefits and shortcomings of each.

4.1   Lightweight and Meta-data only Portals

The first category of geographic data portal is also the simplest. The lightweight or meta-data only portal is more of a catalog than a portal. It simply provides a listing available data sources and their available data type to a user. Figure 8 shows a high level view of the configuration of a lightweight portal and presents how users interact with a lightweight geo-portal.

The interaction steps are labeled in Figure 8, and defined as follows:

1. The portal queries distributed data sources for available data types and meta-data. The portal keeps this listing current, and makes it available to users.
2. Users request and retrieve a listing of data sources, available data types and connection information.
3. Users, with the data source information from the portal, then query each server for the desired data. The queries are executed directly to each data source and are not passed through the portal.

Thus the user has to be able to negotiate the communication protocol of each server listed in the portal.

Table 4-1. Selected OGC Geographic Standards [4]

Standard Name	Description
Web Map Service (WMS)	Provides four protocols in support of the creation and display of registered and superimposed map-like views of information that come simultaneously from multiple sources that are both remote and heterogeneous.
Web Feature Service (WFS)	The purpose of the Web Feature Server Interface Specification (WFS) is to describe data manipulation operations on OpenGIS® Simple Features (feature instances) such that servers and clients can "communicate" at the feature level.
Geography Markup Language (GML)	The Geography Markup Language (GML) is an XML encoding for the transport and storage of geographic information, including both the geometry and properties of geographic features.
Catalog Interface (CAT)	Defines a common interface that enables diverse but conformant applications to perform discovery, browse and query operations against distributed and potentially heterogeneous catalog servers.
Web Coverage Service (WCS)	Extends the Web Map Service (WMS) interface to allow access to geospatial "coverages" that represent values or properties of geographic locations, rather than WMS generated maps (pictures).

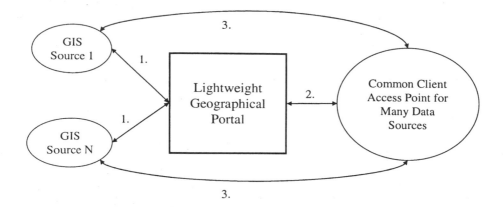

Figure 4-8. System Configuration for Lightweight Portal

An example of a lightweight portal is The National Map by the United States Geological Survey (USGS) The National Map provides a list of sources in XML (extensible markup language). The list is available from this location: http://helios.er.usgs.gov:8080/catprod/start?request=getRecords. The list provides URLs (uniform resource locator) of many data sources and a list of the data types offered by each source. With that list a client can then query directly the servers for the desired data.

There are several benefits of the lightweight portal. First, the workload of the portal is relatively small, because it is only passing metadata to the client and not the actual data. Second, the portal is not limited in the types of sources it lists. Because the portal does not have to actually retrieve data from the sources it can include sources in its catalog without consideration for how the actual data is request, retrieved and interpreted.

However, there are also several disadvantages of this type of integration. First, the client software has to communicate with each data source directly. Thus, it has to implement the communication protocol and query and data formats for each server.

The emergence of new standards for geographical data transfer from the OpenGIS Consortium can mitigate the difficulty of integrating data sources with a variety of interface protocols. However, the data sources have to all implement the standard.

4.2   Heavyweight Portals

The next category of portal is the heavyweight portal. Whereas the lightweight portal provided just a listing of data sources and available data types, the heavyweight portal provides the actual data as well. The diagram in Figure 9 shows a high level view of the configuration of a heavyweight portal.

System interaction steps are labeled in Figure 9, and defined as follows:

1. The portal queries distributed data sources for available data types and meta-data. The portal keeps this listing current, and makes it available to users.
2. Users request and retrieve a listing of data sources, available data types and connection information.
3. Users query the portal for the desired data. The queries are translated from the standard format to that used by a given data source and transmitted to the data source. The response from the data sources is translated from its native format to that used by the portal and send back to the client.

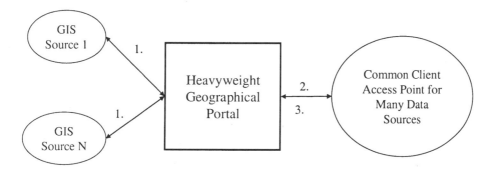

Figure 4-9. System Configuration for Heavyweight Portal

The advantage of this type of system is that client only needs to implement one query and response protocol. The portal converts requests and responses to and from the client into a format understood by the various data sources. Thus all data goes through the portal between the client and the source. The disadvantage is, of course, that the server has to implement communication software for each of the different types of data sources to which it connects.

4.3 Hybrid and Multi-Level Portals

Two final categories of portals are hybrid and multi-level portals. Hybrid portals are those which can act as lightweight and heavyweight portals at the same time. This would be a good solution in the case where some of the connected servers implemented OGC standard protocols and other did not. Those that implemented the standard could be communicated to directly by the client, and those that do not will have communication passed through the portal for translation from native to standard formats. Multi-level portals, as shown in Figure 10, are simply portals that integrate together other portals and make their data available to clients.

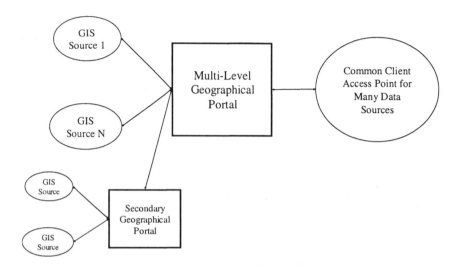

Figure 4-10. System Configuration for Multi-Level Portal

5. THE GEOSPATIAL INFORMATION DATABASE PORTAL SYSTEM

5.1 History

In the previous sections we have described types of geographic data sources and portals. In this section, we will provide a detailed examination of the GIDB. This system has been in development since 1994 and has become something quite different from its original concept. The GIDB started as the first fully object-oriented implementation of several military geographic databases, including Digital Nautical Charts. The GIDB included storage, query and display capabilities in one stand-alone system. However, this platform was quickly stressed beyond its inherent capabilities. Maintaining a large database for each user installation was time consuming and costly. Furthermore, the hardware requirements for each installation were significant. The system had to be capable of running both a full DBMS and a resource intensive client environment.

We began to make changes to the GIDB. First the client software was decoupled from the database and made accessible via the network through CORBA (Common Object Request Brokering Architecture). The client software handled display of the data which was supplied remotely by the database server. At this point, we realized that potential users were very uncomfortable with mapping software that was useless without the network. Only within the last few years, has this changed. Now people expect their mapping software to have a networked component. Users want current data and the only way to provide truly current data is via the network.

The initial decoupling of the client/display software from the database allowed multiple clients to access the same database over the network. Thus, when the database was updated with new data, all users had access to the new data. Furthermore, installation of client software was simplified because the DBMS did not have to be reproduced in each instance.

The next step in the development of the GIDB was to link multiple databases to all GIDB clients. These initial databases included DoD vector and raster mapping products, DoD oceanographic and atmospheric forecast and selected public data sources. Altogether around 5 to 10 local and distributed data sources were part of the initial portal. To facilitate these enhancements extensive changes were made to the GIDB. These changes formed the basis of the current GIDB Portal System. The new architecture opened up many possibilities for data integration. There was now no real limit to the number of databases that could be connected.

One by one additional sources have been added. As of this writing there are over 600 distinct sources of geospatial data dynamically connected to the GIDB. The trend from a system with highly coupled components and detached from the network to an open and expandable system which revolves around the network provides a blueprint for transitioning to a net-centric mindset and framework.

Another trend to note in the development of the GIDB is the move away from commercial software to a combination of open source and government-owned software. The first instance of the GIDB required a costly DBMS and client environment. This expense greatly slowed adoption of the GIDB, because it was prohibitively expensive for all but the a few potential user groups. Slowly, each of the commercial components was replaced with either an open source solution or "in-house" developed software. Thus, the GIDB Portal System is now free of licensing costs.

5.2   Architecture

The GIDB Portal System is unique among geographic data portals, both in the number of data sources available and in the types of data that are connected. Recall the earlier definitions of different types of portals: lightweight, heavyweight, hybrid and multi-level. The GIDB can be classified as all four types. Figure 11 shows high level view of the GIDB architecture.

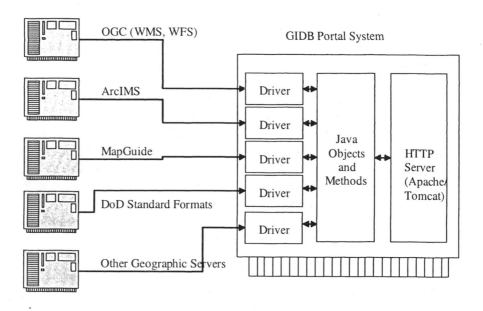

Figure 4-11. High Level View of GIDB Portal System

Note the similarities between this figure and those previously shown to describe generic geographic portal systems. The GIDB links multiple sources and provides a single access point.

5.2.1   Application Server

The core of the GIDB Portal System is the Apache/Tomcat server framework. This configuration was chosen to take advantage of a robust HTTP web server with a Java Servlet engine. The web server component,

Apache, manages network connections with a variety of client software packages. The Java Servlet engine, Tomcat, allows the rich Java library of database, networking, GIS and other components to be used. Apache and Tomcat are both open source software projects and very well supported with frequent program enhancements and security updates.

5.2.2 Database Drivers

Linking data sources within this framework is accomplished by first defining a standard set of data types and query types that encapsulate the functions of a generalized geospatial data server. This standard set in the GIDB is fairly broad. It contains data types for vector and raster map data, meta-data, and extensible user defined data types. Queries based on scale and AOI are provided in addition to methods for acquiring metadata and browsing available data types. This framework constitutes the first level of abstraction in connecting many distributed sources and making them appear as one source. In practical form, the standard set of data types and query methods are defined in a collection of Java classes and interfaces.

This collection of Java classes and interfaces encapsulates all that is required to link a networked data source via a proprietary or custom access protocol to the GIDB. In order to link the external data servers, the data types provided by the server are converted to the GIDB standard format, and the query methods required by the GIDB interface are implemented to function with the query methods provided by the external source.[5] The completed interface between the GIDB and the external interface is called a "driver." The driver also maintains connections to the various data sources. Most of the connected data sources use HTTP based network communication.

A key feature of the GIDB, one that distinguishes it from other solutions, is that all the code and configuration needed to perform the linkage can be located within the GIDB portal system installation. Thus, the provider of the external data source is not required to reconfigure their system in any way. This is the most significant reason for the rapid growth of the number of data servers available in the GIDB. The researchers and developers of the GIDB can configure and catalog data sources around the world without directly interacting with data providers.

The GIDB Portal provides support for data sources which have implemented selected OGC standards, thus servers which provide WMS or WFS services can be quickly and automatically integrated into the GIDB Portal system.

5.3   Interaction Protocols

While each database driver implements communication protocols required to interact with distributed data sources, they also implement a standard set of functions that provide a uniform behavior for servers in the GIDB Portal. Likewise, the drivers produce a standard set of data types to provide a uniform data representation for servers in the GIDB Portal. Thus, GIDB clients only need to be able decode one set of geographic data types.

To better explain how the GIDB Portal functions, we will describe the programmatic methods for interacting with the GIDB. These methods are abstracted through the various GIDB client access methods described in the next section. They are hidden through either a web page, Java application or other tool. Nevertheless, they are behind the scenes in any tool which communicates to the GIDB Portal System.

The GIDB Portal really only implements one external method; this method returns a list of all the available servers that are connected to the GIDB Portal. Each server is represented by a database driver which implements methods to supply the client with a data hierarchy. The data hierarchy is a tree based structure made up of abstract and concrete nodes. Abstract nodes can contain either more abstract nodes or concrete nodes. Concrete nodes represent map data layers which can be requested and retrieved from each geographic data source and provided to a client through the database driver.

We can describe the GIDB Portal as both lightweight and heavyweight, because it is designed such that database drivers can reside either on the portal or they can exist remotely. Thus the GIDB client software packages can receive their data through the portal or directly from the geographic data source, if configured as such.

5.4   Interaction Tools

Previous sections described how different types of data spread out over multiple data sources can be connected and made available through a single source. This section will detail how this single source distributes data to users through a variety of methods. The GIDB standard interface for linking data sources requires that all the data sources be transformed into a common view within the GIDB. Therefore, from a user perspective, the many different data sources do not appear as many sources with many different access protocols; instead, they appear as a single data source with many different categories of data and a single access protocol. [5]

From this point, constructing client software to allow access to the GIDB portal is straightforward. The GIDB framework provides all of the available data types and query methods. The core web/application server provides network access to the GIDB through HTTP. Custom protocols are available for accessing the system, but HTTP is the preferred method for simplicity and ubiquity. There are several client software packages available for accessing the GIDB portal. Table 2 lists the client packages and their benefits. Each client package has access to the same data from a common access point.

Note that OGC standard protocols are listed as client access methods. This is significant. Recall that the GIDB Portal links sources from standards based as well as proprietary sources. With OGC standard output, all the GIDB's data sources are now available in standards based format regardless of their original representation. Thus the GIDB has become an agent for net-centric transformation.

Table 4-2. GIDB Client Software Packages

Client Software Package	Benefits
Web Browser Based "Thin" Client	1. Requires No Installation 2. Simple to Use 3. ISO 19115 Theme Based Data Access
Advanced Client (Full Stand Alone Java Application)	1. Advanced Map Creation Options 2. Includes Encryption and Compression of Mapping Data 3. Includes Ability to Save Generated Maps to Local System 4. Fully Extensible for Data Format, Display, Input and Output
OGC Standard Interfaces (WMS, WFS, etc.)	1. Allows Compatibility with Web services
GIDB API	1. Allows GIDB data sources and themes to be used within independently developed applications

5.5   Data Security

The GIDB Portal system uses Triple Data Encryption Standard (3DES) to secure sensitive data transmissions between the portal and the GIDB thick client. Each server that runs within the GIDB portal has the option of being an "encrypted server". This simply means that one or more 3DES encryption keys are associated with the server. Each encryption key is also associated with a username. When a client attempts to communicate with an encrypted server, the server first checks that a username has been supplied (in plaintext). A key is searched for that matches the given username. If no such key is found, an exception is thrown, communication stops, and the user is given an encryption failure message. Otherwise, all data received from the client after the username is decrypted using the matching key and is then parsed for GIDB Portal commands. If the data from the client was not encrypted (or was encrypted with the wrong key) commands will not be parsable. Encrypted data decrypted with an incorrect key will be gibberish. Responses to the command are encrypted with the same key before being sent back to the client. This scheme requires both client and server to have a copy of the same key file. The key data itself is never transmitted, except when initially given to the client (this happens exactly once, ever, using HTTPS). Encrypted communication then takes place over HTTP just like regular GIDB Portal communication.

Clients request keys for encrypted servers by trying to access the server. The user is prompted for a key file to use for encrypted communications with the server. This same user interface is used to request a key. The client must fill out personal information, which is sent to the server over HTTPS. Once the information is received, the GIDB Portal software automatically emails everyone in the GIDB Portal administrators list, notifying them of the request. After the supplied user information is verified and a determination is made as to whether they have a right to use the encrypted server's data, the request may be granted or denied. The client can then check on their request using the same mechanism, and if granted, will be allowed to download their key file over HTTPS (if the request is denied or still pending they are given the appropriate message). At this point the user can use their key to communicate with the encrypted server.

In the near future this system will most likely be replaced by restricting encrypted servers to accept only communications over HTTPS. Client authentication can then be simpler, requiring only username and password supplied over HTTPS. This should make the encryption scheme more standardized (HTTPS implementations are quite common and scrutinized) and should be more secure (automatic symmetric key changes, symmetric encryption schemes better than 3DES). This scheme was not used in the past because there was not a reliable way to determine if a request to a Java Servlet had been sent over HTTP or over HTTPS (we don't want to hand out sensitive data unless we know with **certainty** that it is going out over a secure connection).

An additional security step is to use PKI (Public Key Infrastructure). This would require each client to have a client certificate issued by a certificate authority. Clients are then authenticated using well-established certificate verification mechanisms to verify that they were granted their certificate from a trusted certificate authority. This is very similar to the HTTPS system mentioned above except that instead of a username and password, the client uses a certificate for authentication. The upside of this scheme is that certificate credentials are much harder to guess than a username and password combination (more data is involved and almost certainly more randomness). The downside of this setup is that each client must have a certificate generated for them by an entity that is potentially not involved in the day to day operation of the GIDB Portal (this could cause long delays in issuing certificates). This problem may be solvable by granting the GIDB Portal certificate authority permission. The client must also have some way to store and access their certificate and securely store and access the associated private key. These added requirements make the system more challenging to implement, but should make it more secure.

Another advantage of PKI is that each piece of data can be tagged or labeled with information that indicates it origin and classification. This provides another level of data assurance. With PKI it is possible to construct a data management system where information can tracked and audited from beginning to end of its cycle.

5.6   Data Presentation

Within the GIDB Thick Client the data is presented in several different ways to suit the needs of different users. This section describes the ways in which the many data sources are presented to users of the GIDB thick client. The first method of presenting data to users is to simply represent every single layer available in the GIDB Portal System. This is literally thousands of layers. However, this is often overwhelming to users, the following three methods represent abstractions intended to simplify the process of finding specific data types within the GIDB Portal.

5.6.1   Theme Based

Instead of listing all the available data sources and layers in one long list, we have adopted an alternative method that presents the layers according to ISO 19115 standard themes [7]. These themes represent the top level presentation of data types to the end user. As an example, under the theme "Biologic and Ecologic Information" in the GIDB the following data layers are listed: Biological Distinctiveness, Ecoregion Divisions, Ecoregion Domains, Ecoregion Provinces, NOAA Mussel Watch, TNC Ecoregions, Terrestrial Ecoregions, Threat to Terrestrial Ecoregions, US Fish & Wildlife Refuges, USGS NDVI Vegetation Index, and WWF Ecoregions. These eleven data layers are representative of over 100 data layers stored in up to seven different data servers. Thus, users of a GIDB client package can quickly get to the required data, with little or no knowledge of the data location or configuration. The list of themes allows users to quickly navigate through the vast amount of data available in the GIDB. This component of the GIDB is called the "Theme Server" and is the most valuable feature to new users.

Much work must be done to make the GIDB Theme Server function effectively. Consider the example in which a user browsing the "Tourism and Recreation" theme selects the "State Park Areas" data layer. If the current map view occupies ten states, then ten servers have to be contacted and ten different data sets have to be requested. The GIDB Theme Server does all this "behind the scenes," and even though the data comes from all over the country, it appears as one source and one layer to the end user. The Theme Server also manages multiple data layers for multiple scales. As a user moves across different map scales, layers are switched to provide the most appropriate data.

For the Theme Server to appropriately link and merge data sets, extensive cataloging of the data must take place ahead of time. This is the most time consuming activity in maintaining the GIDB portal. New servers and data layers are continually appearing and being linked into the system. However, the effort in cataloging and linking in the data sources is well invested. The GIDB portal allows data sources to be configured once and then they are permanently available to all GIDB users.

5.6.2   Sub-Portals

Recently, several other geographic portals have become available on the Internet. Among them are ESRI's Geography Network and USGS's The National Map. These portals offer numerous integrated data sources and are very powerful sources of data. The GIDB Portal has database drivers that can connect to each of these portals and, though they are many distributed data sources, treat them as single sources. In this manner, the GIDB is a multi-level portal or portal of portals. The GIDB Thick client offers users the option of viewing these portals as independent entities.

5.6.3   Search Based Access

The latest addition to the GIDB Portal is the GIDB Search tool. The search tool allows users to perform a keyword search on all layers available in the portal. The following discussion details the novel implementation of the GIDB Search tool.

Each server within the GIDB Portal contains one or more GIS layers. These layers are presented to the user in a multi-tree format. Each server has one or more "root nodes" which can be expanded into their own tree structure with unrestricted numbers of parent and leaf nodes (leaf nodes may also exist at the "root" level). The client program does no caching of these tree structures, other than remaining aware of nodes that are currently expanded by the user. For example, each time a node is collapsed and then re-expanded, a new request is sent to the server to get the node's children. There are some 500 or so servers in the GIDB Portal currently, each with their own metadata trees. This sum of the metadata from all servers would place too much of a burden on the client in terms of memory usage and initial startup time.

The ability to search the metadata in a timely manner requires that all of the metadata be in local memory (local to the search process). For the client to do requests (over HTTP) to search many tree structures (as users do manually) would be far too slow. Multithreading these requests would help at the expense of the server stability but would still be too slow.

The current solution to the problem is to have a process on the server that exhaustively explores the servers and caches their metadata trees. Having this process on the server side allows a single metadata cache to be used by all clients, thus sparing the servers multiple exploration requests from multiple clients.

The server metadata cache consists of an array of root nodes. Each of these root nodes has links to their children and represents a metadata tree from a particular server. Each root is used to seed a vector (a Java class that is essentially an array that can vary in size). An algorithm is then executed to process the vector. It continuously steps through the vector processing of the first node. If the node has children it is removed and the children are put at the end of the vector. If the node is a leaf node, the node is removed from the vector and the node path to the leaf is calculated (each node has a parent link) and converted into an array of words (each node has a name). This word list is then handed to a client-generated search expression (discussed later) and the expression evaluates the word list to determine if it matches the search criteria. This processing continues until the vector is empty, resulting in a complete set of matching node paths. This node path set is returned to the client and can be accessed by the user to add new geographic data layers to the client.

Problems with this scheme include new servers registering with the portal, existing servers deregistering with the portal, and servers modifying their metadata tree structure. The first case is the most common with the other cases being somewhat rare. To solve this problem, the metadata cache process at a given interval (currently 20 minutes), while holding onto and still allowing access to it current cache, reaches out to the various servers and builds a new cache. When the new cache is fully constructed, it is quickly exchanged with the old cache, allowing the search function access to the new/modified data without interrupting search operations that are executing while the new cache is built.

When a client wants to search layers based on some keywords, these keywords and the associated logical operators are turned into an "expression" which is then sent to the server for evaluation against the metadata cache. The simplest expression is a keyword ("road" for instance if the user is interested in road layers). More complex expressions include expressions joined to other expressions using logical operators. These operators are **AND, OR,** and **NOT**, specified in the client using the words "and", "or" and "not" (case insensitive) or the symbols "&&" (**AND**), "&" (**AND**), "||" (**OR**), "|" (**OR**) "!" (**NOT**). The most complex expressions include other expressions nested using parenthesis. The depth of the nesting is unrestricted. The expression, when created, orders its sub-expression evaluation based on nesting level and operator precedence (in the order **NOT, AND, OR**). Some example expressions:

Hydro

"The National Map"

Hydro and "The National Map"

(Hydro and "The National Map") and not Stream

The above examples show how phrases can be searched by enclosing them in quotations (they are then treated as a single keyword). In this case "The National Map" (the name of a server within the GIDB Portal) shows that server names can be searched on, returning all layers from a particular server. Unclosed parentheses are automatically closed. **AND** operators are automatically inserted if no operator is supplied to connect expressions. Various options are also given to the client to allow case matching, full or partial word matching, bounds checking, scale checking, etc. It is truly remarkable how much this search mechanism simplifies providing relevant GIS data to the users.

6.   CONCLUSIONS

The GIDB Portal System has become the leading interconnection of geographic data sources on the Internet. It is flexible in terms of sources to which it can connect and flexible in terms of data presentation. The GIDB Portal comes with a rich set of tools for browsing geographic data. Recent additions to the GIDB Portal, including the GIDB Search tool and the Thematic Server, have made the GIDB Portal simpler and more straightforward to use.

7.   REFERENCES

1. United States Department of Defense, "Net-Centric Data Strategy",May 9,2003, Department of Defense, Chief Information Officer
2. World Wide Web Consortium (November 1, 2004); http:// www.w3.org/2002/ws
3. World Wide Web Consortium (November 1, 2004);http:// www.w3.org/TR/ws-arch/
4. OpenGIS Documents, Retrieved on 1st June, 2004 from the World Wide Web: http:// www.opengis.org/specs/?page=baseline
5. Chung M., R. Wilson, K. Shaw, F. Petry, M. Cobb, "Querying Multiple Data Sources via an Object-Oriented Spatial Query Interface and Framework", *Journal of Visual Languages and Computing* Vol. 12, No. 1, pp. 37-60, February 2001.
6. Wilson, R., M. Cobb, F. McCreedy, R. Ladner, D. Olivier, T. Lovitt, K. Shaw, F. Petry, M. Abdelguerfi, "Geographical Data Interchange Using XML-Enabled Technology within the GIDB System", Chapter 13, *XML Data Management*, Akmal B. Chaudhri, editor, Addison-Wesley, Boston, 2003.
7. Peng, Zhong-Ren and Ming-Hsiang Tsou, *Internet GIS:Distributed Geographic Information Services for the Internet and Wireless Network,* Wiley and Sons, Hoboken, New Jersey, 2003.

Chapter 5

ANALYZING INTELLIGENCE DATA
Next Generation Technologies for Connecting the Dots

Christopher R. Westphal
Visual Analytics, Inc. 20010 Fisher Avenue, 2nd Floor, Poolesville, MD 20837
westphal@visualanalytics.com

Abstract: The IT boom of the 1990's left many organizations and companies awash in data. With the popularity of the Internet, data sets were collected on virtually every topic, for every purpose, for every mouse-click, for every reason imaginable. Often, multiple databases or huge data warehouses were built to store these immense quantities of data. Although billions of dollars are spent every year to collect and store information, data owners paradoxically often spend only pennies on analysis. What has been missing from the IT landscape is a way in which all of the data can be effectively analyzed – a way to connect-the-dots. Without a means to use and understand the data that has been collected, the owners of the data will never realize the potential benefits of these resources. This has already been evidenced with the events of 9/11 and the government's limited effort to share, combine, analyze, and report on the pre- and post-indicators. This chapter discusses the next generation information sharing and analytical systems that are being created and deployed to overcome these issues to better address terrorism, money laundering, narcotics trafficking, and fraud investigations.

Key words: Visualization, Link Analysis, Collaboration, Network Mining, Information Sharing, Link Charts, Virtual Data Warehouse, Association Graphs

1. INTRODUCTION

Since the disastrous events of September 11th, governments and businesses around the world are operating in a state of heightened security and awareness of the possibility of additional terrorist attacks. While these unfortunate events changed our lives forever, these events have also alerted us to the dangers of fanatical individuals and groups who are willing to go to any lengths and face any and all consequences for what they believe. This situation has caused government agencies and corporations to focus more seriously on issues of security, collaborative analyses and information sharing. These themes have been repeatedly emphasized by many top officials in the world's leading democratic governments and private industries because terrorism and similar threats are an international concern.

In light of these and other events, it has become increasingly clear that the intelligence community is not a collaborative set of organizations. In fact, the reality is that there has been little sharing of intelligence information between agencies. Had there been a more collaborative atmosphere between intelligence agencies and better analytical systems in place, September 11th might have been avoided. This has caused the government to seek new tools and techniques that allow faster, better and more effective ways of understanding and analyzing data contained within home agencies, as well as data contained in the databases of other agencies.

Corporations are also operating on a heightened sense of awareness to external and internal threats to their business. Critical areas of analysis, like fraud detection in the banking and insurance and health care industries must utilize better and more powerful systems to detect the anomalies and patterns contained in their data sources – e.g., they must work smarter. Other areas of analysis such as understanding consumer spending patterns are becoming increasingly important as firms attempt to maximize revenues through targeted marketing and cross selling.

As companies become increasingly aware of their vulnerabilities, they look for new ways to identify, quantify and protect themselves from the huge losses that fraud and security breaches can engender. Others want to stay abreast or ahead of their competition in the marketplace by managing their data more efficiently to discover improvements in their business processes and activities.

All of these scenarios and situations are based on the ability to effectively access, integrate, and analyze data to expose new patterns.

2.   SHARING DATA

Sharing data is not a new concept nor is it technically difficult. In fact, the capabilities have been in place for quite some time. It is somewhat ironic that freeware such as Napster, Gnutella, Morpheus, BearShare, and KaZaA is readily downloadable from the Internet and allows millions of people across the globe to share files, documents, pictures, videos, and music with the click of a button; while the intelligence community and law enforcement agencies have little capability or impetus to share information. Many of the obstacles are due to the limitations on the application of the technologies required to facilitate the analyses and some can be attributed to politics, stovepipe systems, isolated processes, or compartmented procedures that dominate how these organizations operate.

The analytical landscape has changed over the past decade. Traditional approaches were focused around processing standardized reports and fixed types of output. However, the amount of data currently being generated far exceeds the capacity to analyze even a small percentage of it. Many organizations and agencies have been collecting data for long periods of time and have built up vast databases, information stores, and data warehouses.

The goal is to determine how to "connect the dots" in these data repositories to discover the important patterns and relationships. It is such a simple concept – connect the dots. In fact, many children play this game early in their development process as part of learning their ABCs or numbers. Each correct connection between a set of points reveals more of a hidden pattern. As long as the correct sequence of numbers or letters is followed, the final diagram is eventually completed – exposing the "big picture." How hard can it be?

As we have all heard from post-9/11 analyses, there were plenty of indicators to follow based on known processes or suspicious activities. For example, we learned that if someone enters the country on a student visa, then attends flight training for commercial aircraft, and has indirect linkages to known terrorists; they are most likely a prime target for a follow-up investigation. Connect the dots – the picture is clear, right?

Unfortunately, to connect the dots would indicate that we already know the pattern and it would be a simple matter of generating a query to report on all known instances of the pattern. Hindsight plays an important role in exposing certain patterns that were previously unknown. Thus, we must constantly ask ourselves:

- What does a terrorist look like?
- What does a money launderer look like?
- What does a criminal look like?
- What does a fraudster look like?

The data available to answer these questions can determine what "dots" need to be connected. In many instances the data is not readily available, is controlled by a different group, or does not contain the proper information. So the question becomes: what is the sequence or order in which the dots are connected and what happens when there are missing dots?

The templates (or rules) ultimately created to derive the answers (e.g., connect the dots) will be based on known scenarios and can certainly be automated wherever possible. However, the real threat lies in the "unknown." Changes in the existing patterns or different approaches to circumventing the systems will ultimately compromise the templates that are in place. Instead of airline training, the subjects apply for commercial driving licenses or explosive permits, purchase large storage containers, or simply rent a truck. Will the existing templates flag these events? Will the data be available? Will the analyst know what to look for?

It is critical that the analytical methodologies employed in these types of environments be able to find different variations in the patterns of interest. Any templates defined to help expose probable targets of interest should ultimately be reviewed by a human analyst to determine if the template was properly applied – and most importantly, to determine if there are any exceptions to the rule. The results must always be verified and should never be determined 100% by computer algorithms.

A good example of this occurred when developing a data-centric application for the Department of Treasury. In this particular application a number of different data sources (over a dozen) were being integrated for a particular area in the Southeastern region of the United States. Two of the sources processed activated on a "subject" resulting in a well-qualified target; a high-value asset (a residence worth over US$1M) with a low reported means of income (less than US$10,000).

In this scenario, the house was located in a very affluent suburb of Atlanta with a market value of over $1.5 million and the subject had a reported income of only $4,000. Needless to say, the system performed according to expectations. Once identified, Special Agents performed a more thorough review to confirm the circumstances of the pattern and quickly discovered additional "dimensions" to the pattern that were unexposed. As it turns out, the pattern triggered on one of the children where the amount was the total interest reported from a savings account. The father, with the same name, had reported the income to afford/support the residence.

In this case, the rules were perfectly valid and exposed circumstances that would normally result in an active investigation; however, there are always exceptions to the rule(s) as this scenario indicated. The due diligence performed by the Special Agents avoided a situation that could have gotten unpleasant, at best.

3. CONNECT THE DOTS

State and local law enforcement agencies have always been looking for a better "mousetrap" to use in conducting their investigations. Often, a lone investigator tirelessly searches through the clues putting all of the pieces together to solve the crime. Each clue is critical in and of itself, but more important is knowing how each applies to the overall case. Traditionally,

Law Enforcement Agencies (LEAs) have not been proficient with advanced technologies such as database systems, data visualization, and rule-bases – although that is changing as more highly-trained investigators are coming up through the ranks. Data-centric technologies have been deployed in a variety of LEAs to help them better understand their case data, integrate data sets, and pursue leads.

Law enforcement is a unique challenge in the analytical world because each organization operates independently while trying to achieve the common and collective goal of combating crime. Although politics and arrest credits all play into how much one agency is willing to support the sharing of their resources, it has been observed that many embrace capabilities to make more effective use of their resources. Collaborative data sharing among different agencies is an idea whose time has come and represents a win-win situation for all involved. Currently there are a growing number of programs that have targeted the incorporation of information sharing technologies into their underlying architectures.

The following example and related diagrams show how an investigator might pursue a case where multiple sources of data are accessed across a variety of different agencies. Usually, there is a known starting point from a past crime, arrest, or some type of situation. This type of investigation typically represents a "reactive" situation.

Reactive analyses are based on the pre-selection of an entity such as a person (as in this case), organization, account, location, shell casing, DNA sample, or event. The entity of interest is already known and becomes the center, or focus, of the analysis. Ultimately, the goal of a reactive analysis is to expand the network to find additional clues and leads. In our example, the investigator would look at all aspects of the subject to determine what other people are related through family, business dealings, criminal records, or any other source, to show unusual connections or associations that may possibly show important connections to other criminal activities. Indirect relationships through addresses, phone numbers, or vehicles would also be pursued by the investigator.

Following the path of connections, additional entities can be identified based on their connection(s) to the original entity. To maintain the context of the analysis, any new entities then become the source for the next level of inquiry. The investigator has the option to append or replace the current working data set with new data to control how much or how little information will be displayed for any given subject.

The first source utilized in this example is based on criminal arrest data, usually provided by the local police department, where a subject with the name "Brad Billings" is currently under suspicion of criminal activity. The

entity shown is depicted with a specific date of birth used to help distinguish
him from other people with exact or similar names.

BILLINGS
BRAD
05/01/1956

Figure 5-1. The Suspect

Keep in mind that many organizations and agencies that collect
information often do not fully understand how the data will be used or
analyzed. The real challenge is in improving the accuracy of the data through
better collection and representation methods. In this case, the only uniquely
identifying information is the combination of the name and date of birth.

Needless to say, this can lead to problems as experienced by Senator
Edward Kennedy (Massachusetts) during the summer of 2004 when he was
stopped while boarding airline flights on five different occasions because his
name was matched to an entry on a government no-fly-list. Additionally,
Congressman John Lewis (Georgia) claimed that he was also required to
commit to additional security checks because his name was matched on a
watch list. In both cases, the data processed by these systems represented
only a limited portion of what was necessary to properly perform an
appropriate match.

Another good example regarding the collection and representation of data
is based on systems that have been deployed into Korea utilizing advanced
data mining technologies. In Korea, it is nearly impossible to target/analyze
data utilizing the name of a subject. With a population of approximately 45
million people, it is estimated that over 20% share the same last name of
"Kim." Thus, an alternative primary reference, such as their Resident
Registration Number loosely translated as "Jumin deungrok beonho," is
often used to uniquely identify people in Korea. The Resident Registration
Number, which is similar to the U.S. Social Security Number, is a 13 digit
number based on a combination of birth date, gender, and registration related
data (region/order).

In continuing with the example, Figure 2 shows the first level of
connections, revealing that the subject has relationships to a variety of
different objects including a criminal organization called the Outlaws Gang.
There is also a criminal file (shown as the folder icon) that contains all of the
details, dates, times, locations, and descriptions associated with the case.

Additionally, the subject's driver's license, Social Security Number (SSN), phone number, and last known address are depicted in this diagram.

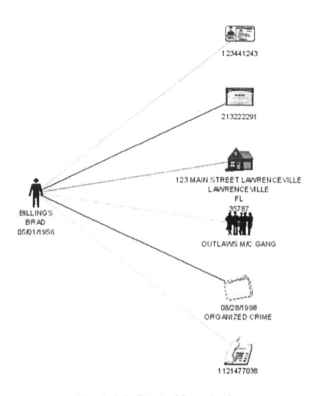

123441243

213222291

123 MAIN STREET LAWRENCEVILLE
LAWRENCEVILLE
FL
35787

OUTLAWS M/C GANG

08/28/1998
ORGANIZED CRIME

1121477038

BILLINGS
BRAD
05/01/1956

Figure 5-2. Criminal Investigation

Additional searches to try and identify any associates, gang members, or family members living at the same address come up negative from the criminal database. Thus, there is no other information present in this particular source that will further extend the network. However, because this agency has access to other sources of data, the investigator cross-references all of the information into another online source. In this example the phones, ID numbers, and addresses are checked against a federal database containing all Suspicious Activity Reports (SARs) filed by banks, financial institutions, casinos, and money service businesses (MSBs) throughout the United States.

On January 1, 2002, as part of the changes enacted by the U.S. Patriot Act, requirements went into effect for MSBs to submit SARs. According to the U.S. Department of the Treasury, an MSB is defined as a money transmitter or issuer, or seller or redeemer of money orders or traveler's checks, which also includes the U.S. Postal Service. MSBs are required to report suspicious activity within 30 days by filing the SAR-MSB Form when a transaction (or series of transactions) exceeds $2,000 and is believed to be derived from illegal activity, serves no business or apparent lawful purpose, or is attempting to evade any requirements of the Bank Secrecy Act (BSA).

The basic business process of MSBs is to transfer money within a network of authorized agents. There is always a sender and a receiver of the money and reviewing the flow of money between the actual participants (e.g., the subjects) in the network is the basis for performing money laundering investigations. However, it is also a duty of the MSB to monitor the individual agents to ensure they remain compliant with their reporting requirements and are not trying to circumvent any controls within the system. In 2003, there were over 150,000 independent, local, and multi-national businesses within the United States, classified as an MSB, that filed over 200,000 SAR MSBs.

Figure 3 shows that a match was made in the SAR-MSB database on the driver's license number. As it turns out, our suspect was involved in three separate suspicious financial transactions (shown as SAR icons) where the driver's license number was listed along with a different Social Security Number, a different phone number, and a partial address which appears to match the first address. Interestingly, our suspect also listed a different date of birth during these transactions resulting in a new icon depicting the differences.

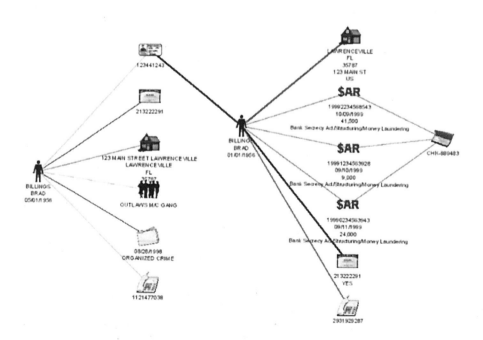

Figure 5-3. Money Laundering

The quality (consistency, correctness, and precision) of data impacts the accuracy and reliability of analytical and monitoring systems. In the financial industry, the data are prone to virtually every type of misrepresentation imaginable. Simple mistakes such as spelling errors, phonetic interpretations, or abbreviations account for a large number of the inconsistent data recorded.

In one financial database analyzed, a large, well-known west coast city was entered with 13 different spellings, a venerable bank had 18 unique name variations, and the number of permutations for certain industry occupations (e.g., chef, cook, waiter, worker at a restaurant, etc.) were almost unmanageable. Also, under the circumstances, most people will not be entirely truthful with their information while others will outright lie or intentionally misrepresent themselves to the financial institution.

In a recent analysis of I-94 data (international arrival/departure records), an individual was targeted because he had 56 different passport numbers used in over 200 flights made from/to a foreign country (Mexico) over the course of a single year. This volume of travel is somewhat expected for a person in his line of business as an international courier, however the number of misrepresentations made on recording his passport number, whether accidental or intentional, occurred so frequently that it could not be overlooked. Most of the variations came from the data entry process where the numbers 2 and 5, 4 and 9, and 1 and 7 can be easily mistaken or transposed (especially when dealing with bad penmanship). The good news in this particular case was that the poor quality of the data actually worked in favor of the investigators to expose his actions.

In continuing with the investigation, the thicker linkages (shown in Figure 3) between the displayed entities indicates that the driver's license, Social Security Number, address, and telephone were all consistently listed for each of the three suspicious transactions. Thus, the investigator has a degree of confidence that he is still targeting the same suspect from the criminal investigation. Of further interest is that all the transactions occurred on the same account. This entity becomes the focus of the next inquiry made by checking for any wire transfers made against that account.

Figure 4 shows that there are 10 transactions (wires) performed on this account. Each wire was a deposit for an amount less than $10,000. A quick review of the transfer dates showed they occurred within a few weeks of one another. Most likely, a counterpart (c.g., another gang member) in a different city wired the proceeds of criminal activity, such as narcotics trafficking, prostitution, or extortion, to the account maintained by our suspect.

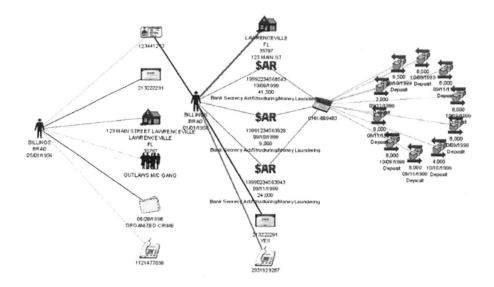

Figure 5-4. Wire Transfers

The bank became suspicious of these wire transfers and filed SARs on the suspect when he came to withdraw the money from this account. From this information, the investigator concludes the money is most likely being used to fund the operations of the criminal organization (e.g., the Outlaws Gang). Unfortunately, the investigator has no additional suspects at this time so he turns to search some other sources that relate to the criminal case associated with the suspect.

At this point in the investigation, the focus turns to the telephone numbers associated with the subject. Often during investigations, pen registers and trap/trace devices are used to record the numbers dialed to/from a phone. Additionally, the phone companies maintain very accurate call records that can be obtained through court orders.

Ultimately an investigator can obtain Title III phone intercepts to listen to the actual calls once there is enough justification and a court order signed by a judge to warrant this type of approach. An interesting note about Title IIIs is that there are privileged conversations that are excluded from monitoring, including those between the attorney/client, husband/wife, priest/penitent, and doctor/patient, unless the privilege has been waived or there are discussions regarding criminal activities.

Figure 5 shows there are a number of different phone numbers that are indirectly connected to our suspect's phone. In this case, the thicker linkages indicate more frequent communication (e.g., more phone calls) between the two numbers. Often in the narcotics trade, there are trust relationships built up between the different players where communications for product and payment are discussed regularly. Although phone numbers are commonly discarded to help avoid being tracked, our current suspect has used his number exclusively to call a "lieutenant" in the gang to coordinate their activities.

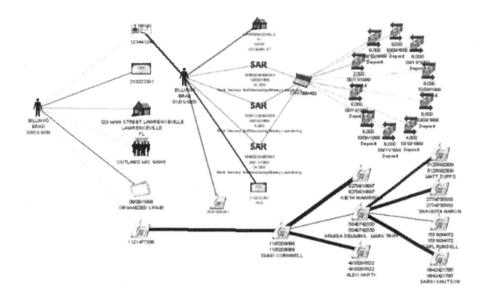

Figure 5-5. Telephone Tolls

The network of phone calls expands for three levels. Each new phone number will have to be individually verified to determine the subscriber and their role in the gang or other related entity. Using this type of representation, the investigator gets an understanding of how a phone interacts with other phones; what is does not tell the investigator is the pattern of interaction among the phones. Generally, there will be some type of temporal component (i.e., time and date) associated with the event (e.g., the phone call) that can be used to establish a pattern.

When detecting temporal behaviors, one must reflect on the type of data that are available for supporting such patterns. Typically, we think about "transactional" events such as financial deposits and withdrawals, border crossings, credit card purchases, travel events, terrorist actions, narcotics dealing, and of course, telephone tolls. The common thread between all transactions is that they support a time/date characteristic.

Usually a single transaction is not significant, however, when all transactions are viewed collectively for a specific type of data (e.g., a phone number, a credit card, an account) we can infer behavior based on how the transactions occurred. Viewing transactions in the context of other transactions can lead to some very interesting results.

The patterns exposed through a temporal analysis will show when the phone calls tend to occur. Examples would include every Tuesday between 2:00 and 3:00 (absolute) or phone-x calls phone-y only after a call from phone-z (sequential). In this example, the investigator is only interested in exposing additional subjects to pursue and therefore is only interested in how the phones connect with one another.

The final step in this investigation is to target additional suspects, which is achieved by checking local Department of Motor Vehicles (DMV) records. In this state, the residential phone number for a registered vehicle connects to the owner who, in turn, connects to an address and vehicle (identified by a VIN). Figure 6 show a representation of how the data is presented.

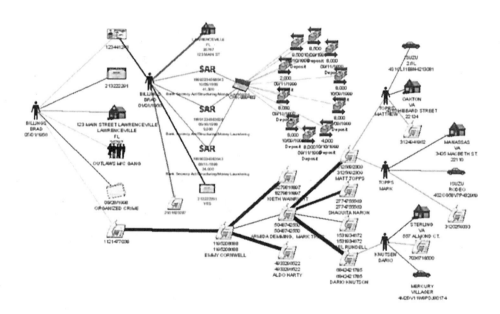

Figure 5-6. Vehicle Registrations

For this investigation, additional subjects are revealed including two brothers who live in separate towns within the Washington, DC area. They are connected through the same home phone number even though their addresses are different. The ultimate goal of the investigator is to connect the dots and expose as many potential targets as possible and then select the most "well qualified target" for additional review and follow-up.

State and local agencies can provide a wide range of data – from real-property and utility records to driver's licenses and criminal arrests. The volumes of data maintained by state and local governments provide more detail (resolution) on individuals to help round out data collected at the federal level. Furthermore, information providers such as ChoicePoint, LexisNexis, Qsent, and others, are invaluable resources in providing timely access across a large number of different sources. Other private sources of data including rental car companies, commercial airlines, and banks can also be used to gain a better understanding of certain subjects.

4. ANALYTICAL VERSUS REFERENTIAL DATA

As was seen in the previous example, five sources of data were effectively combined to expose important patterns of interest and help connect the dots. The sources used in this example represented "analytical sources" such that individually, they could all be analyzed independently of one another. However, there are sources of data used to supplement the analysis that are defined as *referential*, meaning they contain no analytical value, only supplemental information with respect to the analytical sources.

A referential source is used almost exclusively to determine if specific characteristics exist for certain objects and usually do not support the ability to expose relationships or networks themselves. Speed permitting, referential sources are often included as an additional dataset that are typically accessed in a passive fashion when the investigator previews the data. For example, if any of the people in the prior example were wanted on outstanding warrants, they could be flagged with a special icon indicating a prior murder, narcotics conviction, or money laundering indictment. The importance of this fact would be shown graphically as the checks were made automatically in the background by the system.

To provide an example of this type of information, there exists a reference database of all financial investigations that were conducted by a particular Federal Agency and their associated Document Control Numbers (DCNs). Every case represented in this database of approximately 100,000 entries consists of one or more unique control numbers (referenced as the TRANSFER object) that can be matched against the main data source. The control number defines the original source, the date of the filing, and a unique sequence number. When a match is found, the case ID from the reference source is added as an attribute to the TRANSFER object and its primary image is overridden with a "special" icon as shown in Figure 7.

Figure 5-7. Referential Case

In another example, the reference source is the Social Security Death Master Index (SSDM) that is acquired from the U.S. government (surprisingly from the Department of Commerce). This source has almost 100,000,000 records of people who are deceased and have received a death benefit from the government. The record format is fairly basic and contains the Social Security Number, last/first/middle name, date of birth, date of death, and region of death. For any database utilizing an SSN, the SSDM can be checked and matches shown for anyone conducting financial transactions with the SSN of a deceased person. If a match is found, the icon for the SSN, as shown in Figure 8, can be changed to reflect this fact and the analyst can investigate further.

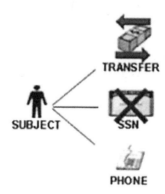

Figure 5-8. Death Master Reference

In this last example, a State Attorney General's Office annually subpoenas all of the public payphones within the state to obtain their phone numbers, operating organizations, and physical locations. This database contains over 45,000 entries and is used as a reference source to determine if people have listed payphones as either their home or work phone number when conducting financial transactions, providing criminal arrest data, or applying for welfare/food stamps. When a match is encountered in the payphone reference database the PHONE icon is changed (see Figure 9) to reflect this situation and the investigator then has a well-qualified target to pursue.

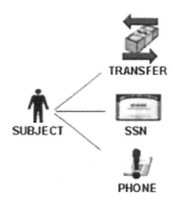

Figure 5-9. Public Payphone Reference

5. VIRTUAL DATA WAREHOUSE

In the post-9/11 era, many organizations have expressed the need to share data in order to "connect the dots" and to see the bigger picture. A number of systems, networks, and approaches have been deployed to help provide this capability to the community. Until now, the progress has been somewhat limited and in the years that have passed, many agencies are still not actively sharing information.

A variety of different approaches have been proposed to address this problem including one recent and highly publicized project by the U.S. government that wanted to "copy" information from virtually every law and government agency into a behemoth, nationwide data warehouse where it would be analyzed by experts and properly disseminated through appropriate channels. The concept is simple – to bring it all together in one place where it could be collectively analyzed. This approach presents many technical challenges that must be overcome including data aggregation, scalability, security, sheer physical storage of the masses of information, and issues associated with control and accountability.

What happens when 100's or 1000's of data sources can be accessed and queried simultaneously? A different approach and methodology are required to provide members within a community the means to easily share their information without the headache or overhead associated with a massive data warehouse. A distributed architecture, similar to the peer-to-peer systems mentioned previously, can be used to allow organizations to selectively and securely share data with others.

In a distributed model, information (databases, documents, etc.) can stay in its current location, eliminating the need to copy to new locations for the sake of "integration." This approach has been termed a "Virtual Data Warehouse" and provides a common sense approach to data sharing, which can be implemented on very large scales connecting hundreds or thousands of data sources. This distributed system approach has many advantages over its conventional counterpart including security, real-time access, and robustness.

- Security - Consider access control with regard to data sharing. In part, this means keeping data safe from unauthorized access and regulating that access to appropriate segments of information depending on the user. For instance, organization "X" may have 10 databases and 2 million documents it wants to make available to its own local users and several external organizations with their own groups of users. Further, some of these databases are sensitive within organization "X" such that only a small group of users can see them. A granular security model is needed that enforces the permissions for each data source. Additionally, the security model itself must also support a distributed approach where organization "X" can delegate some authority for sharing its data to administrators in remote organizations whom they trust to apply appropriate permissions to their users.
- Real-Time Access - The nature of a distributed system lends itself to real-time information access. Consider a data warehouse approach where information from many sources must be copied into a centralized warehouse. Depending on the methods used, each of these sources may be copied at various intervals ranging from hours to days to weeks. In contrast, the distributed model doesn't need to copy data because it connects to the "live" data providing real-time, peer-to-peer data sharing. If any of these services worked off of a static, clumsy, centralized data repository, the service would not be dynamic, or very useful to many users.
- Robustness - Consider a system where data from 50 sites around the nation is copied to a single location, then searched and analyzed remotely by users from those same 50 sites. What happens if that single location becomes unavailable? Potentially, hundreds or thousands of users will be

offline because that single location is a single point of failure. Now, consider that same data in the same 50 locations where instead of copying data, each of the 50 locations offered a data sharing hub that enabled secure sharing to both local users and each of 49 affiliate locations. This model is much more robust because there is no single point of failure for the entire system. Moreover, the entire system of 50 locations is real-time and each location retains full control over the dissemination of their data.

Additionally, using a traditional data warehouse approach requires that the format of the data be changed into a single composite representation. This makes users subject to the decisions made by a remote party which may not reflect their particular needs. In a distributed approach, each format remains intact while utilizing access and transformation features to add value to the end results.

In a distributed environment, each server can broker a search or other request on behalf of an authenticated user to another server in an affiliate organization. Information sent between servers can be encrypted and sent via the HTTP (SOAP/XML) protocol in order to help traverse firewalls that exist between different locations. This means that users in one location will be able to search for and analyze data that physically resides in multiple locations. This type of integrated technology is unprecedented and considered mandatory in the next-generation analytical systems.

Although agencies have shared data using other types of remote data access including terminal emulations, web portals, or specialized applications/protocols, the use of a real-time, distributed approach for creating a virtual data warehouse is somewhat of a novel approach for government and law enforcement organizations. The owners of the data control who is allowed access and how much they are allowed to see for any given request. Requests are made from a network of distributed servers that are responsible for the authentication, security, and load balancing of the system. This approach allows for n-way sharing of data where any number of agencies can share data thereby allowing for data producers, consumers, or both.

The following topics should be considered when sharing data:
1. Avoid the creation of a centralized warehouse: The resources necessary to consolidate data can be expensive and time consuming. Using a virtual warehouse through a distributed data sharing model provides a more flexible, adaptable, and scalable system.
2. Utilize existing data formats and layouts: Systems should be capable of mapping to the existing database schemas and formats. Very little, if any, preprocessing of the data should be required to prepare data for sharing.

3. Automate accounting: Systems should have a strong accounting model such that all data requests are logged into a separate data repository that can be reviewed and reported on for security, case support, or deconfliction. Accounting must be enabled at each source/site by the owner of the data.
4. Manage the volume and detail returned: Reasonable limitations should be placed on the amount and type of information returned by each query to avoid overburdening resources and limit abuse. Pointer indexes should be used when sensitive data can't be generically shared.
5. Control access: System access should always be controlled by the owner of the data. Those sites that post a source of data should remain in total control over who gains access, the type of access, and the volume of data returned.

As agencies start to reap the benefits of sharing data, they can also expect the quality of the results, analyses, and reports to improve dramatically. The costs associated with many types of operations can be reduced because the manpower required to access and collect the information can be minimized. Additionally, duplication of efforts such as hosting the same sources, performing the same analytics, and generating the same reports can be curtailed thereby freeing up more resources to perform other work. The ROI (return on investment) for information sharing is immediate, significant, and measurable.

6.   CONCLUSION

The analytical community is changing every day. New methods, approaches, and technologies are being applied to help facilitate how data is accessed, combined, analyzed, and reported. This is a never-ending and constantly changing paradigm where new techniques and methods must be developed to keep pace with the threats that emerge everyday. Terrorism has changed how governments and businesses operate and our adversaries are constantly changing how they will plan and execute the next attack. Information sharing is key to facilitating better analytics. Over the next decade there will be massive efforts to clean up, standardize, and share data. Already in the works are the creation of fusion systems, analytical centers, and collaborative task forces – all designed to connect-the-dots.

7.   REFERENCES

For additional reading on analytical methodologies and link analysis systems, read:
  Westphal, C.R. (1998). *Data Mining Solutions* (with T. Blaxton), John Wiley & Sons, New York, NY.

Visit the following URLs for more detail on analytical results:
  http://support.visualanalytics.com/Newsletter/
  http://www.visualanalytics.com/Products/VLinkChart/index.cfm

For information on public data sources available online across the United Sates, visit:
  http://www.searchsystems.net

Chapter 6

LINKING MILITARY SYSTEMS WITH SIMULATIONS AND INTELLIGENT AGENTS THROUGH WEB SERVICES TO SUPPORT COURSES OF ACTION ANALYSIS

Ranjeev Mittu
U.S. Naval Research Laboratory, Information Technology Division, Advanced Information Technology Branch, 4555 Overlook Avenue, SW, Washington, DC 20375

Abstract: The Department of Defense (DoD) has begun to invest resources to support the development of the Global Information Grid (GIG), a plug-and-play Service Oriented Architecture (SOA) whose goal is to enable interoperability between network-centric entities. This chapter describes the current state-of-the-art in web services technology and its role in the GIG. It then discusses a GIG prototype supporting the web-service enabled interoperability between a military system, simulation and intelligent agents for Course of Action Analysis (CoAA). Next, this chapter addresses challenges for agents in the GIG, as well as potential limitations in the use of web services. This chapter concludes with a survey of competing technologies that may help overcome the limitations and provides a brief summary, including future research areas with regard to the GIG prototype.

Key words: Course of Action, Military Systems, Simulations, Intelligent Agents, Multi-agent Systems, Plan Monitoring, Global Information Grid, Web Services, Peer-to-Peer Computing, World Wide Web

1.   INTRODUCTION

Web Services technology is gaining momentum and maturing rapidly within the World Wide Web Consortium (W3C) [34], and has the potential to provide the infrastructure necessary to support a SOA such as the GIG. Web services are services that are made available from a business's Web server for Web users or other Web-connected programs. The primary components that comprise web services include the Universal Description and Discovery Interface (UDDI), Web Services Description Language (WSDL) and Simple Object Access Protocol (SOAP). These three technologies are generally used together in a coordinated fashion to support the discovery of, and interaction with, web services. Furthermore, there are a number of supporting technologies, such as the Business Process Execution Language (BPEL)[1] and Ontology Web Language for Services (OWL-S) [1], which complement the primary web service components. These supporting technologies have the potential to add additional value in SOA environments by providing capabilities that enable the management of services. The BPEL provides constructs for composing complex service transactions based on the interactions and linkages between simpler services. The OWL-S, like BPEL, also enables service composition. However, it also provides additional constructs for describing the necessary service semantics in order to intelligently reason about what is being offered by the service. Both BPEL and OWL-S will be described later in the chapter.

The DoD has begun to invest resources to support the development of the GIG [13], a plug-and-play SOA whose goal is to enable interoperability between network-centric entities. These entities will include not only military platforms and supporting software applications, but also intelligent agents, which may be required to assist users/applications in managing the information available on the GIG. The underlying technology that is envisioned to provide the backbone of the GIG will be web services. The GIG infrastructure will enable the dynamic interconnectivity and interoperability between all levels of military entities, and is a shift from more traditional military architectures such as the Defense Information Infrastructure (DII) Common Operating Environment (COE) [8]. The DII COE is considered a *"stovepiped"* architecture, as the interface points between systems or software components are not easily reconfigurable.

There are many definitions of software agents in the literature, but a general definition of a software agent according to [33] is *"a computer system that is situated in some environment, and that is capable of autonomous action in this environment in order to meet its design objective"*. Multi-agent Systems employ groups of software agents that cooperate with each other to accomplish a given set of tasks (see text box on the following page)

---

[1] Also known as Business Process Execution Language for Web Services (BPEL4WS)

The field of AI can be broadly categorized in terms of three sub-fields: *distributed problem solving, parallel AI* and *multi-agent systems*. Distributed problem solving takes a top-down approach; the problem is decomposed into smaller problems, which are assigned to software modules that compute the individual solutions which are then combined by some higher level process into a global solution. The field of parallel AI deals with performance and resource utilization in problem solving. The field of multi-agent systems deals with a bottom-up approach, which assumes that agents will cooperate with each other to negotiate tasks that need to be solved, while cooperating or resolving conflicts. Invariably, there may be many definitions of what constitutes *intelligence*. For example, agents able to reason about their environment or learn through interaction with their environment, other agents or through users might be considered *intelligent*.

The intelligent agents operating within the GIG may be expected to support users and applications in intelligently discovering and processing information, while coordinating with similar agents as necessary to support these processes. It is reasonable to expect that the efficiency of individual agents (in terms of locating and filtering information in the GIG) may be increased through cooperation and subsequent teamwork with other agents.

This remainder of this chapter will be organized as follows: Section 2 will describe the state-of-the-art in web service technology. Section 3 will discuss the development of the GIG, and how web services will be one of the enabling technologies that will be the foundation for the GIG. Section 4 will describe a proof-of-principle that is being developed to showcase the interoperability between a military system, simulation and software agents to support CoAA. The interconnectivity between each of these components is being developed to leverage web service technology. The goal of this prototype is to demonstrate the coupling of simulations with military Command and Control systems to assist in the detection of critical deviations in a plan's execution as reported to the military system. Intelligent agents are responsible for detecting the deviations between reported movements and the simulated movements and alerting the user. The user then has the option to use the services offered by the simulation to spawn multiple "what-if" scenarios to explore CoAA. Section 5 will discuss the challenges agents may face in the GIG. Section 6 will describe potential limitations in the use of web service technology within the GIG, while section 7 provides a brief survey of competing technologies that may help overcome some of the limitations. Lastly, in section 8, we provide a brief summary.

2.   WEB SERVICES

Web service technology is rapidly gaining momentum under the auspices of the W3C. The W3C was established in 1994 to help lead the development of standards, specifications, guidelines, software, etc, to promote the evolution and interoperability of the World Wide Web (WWW).   Web services technology includes three key components that are used in conjunction with each other. These components include the UDDI, WSDL and SOAP.   It should be noted that UDDI is not the only registry standard. For example, the ebXML [9] Registry and Repository Standard is sponsored by the Organization for the Advanced of Structured Information Standards (OASIS) and the United Nations Center for the Facilitation of Procedures and Practices in Administration, Commerce and Transport.   The UDDI, however, has emerged as the registry standard for the GIG.

The UDDI is a framework that defines XML-based registries in which businesses can upload information about themselves and the services they offer. An XML-based registry contains names of organizations, services provided by those organizations, and descriptions about service capabilities. XML registries based on the UDDI specification provide common areas through which systems/organizations can advertise themselves and their web services.   Attributes that can be registered include the description of the organization that agrees to provide the service as well as information about specific points of contact (including their phone number and email addresses). The UDDI registries also contain information about services as well as service bindings (which are needed to connect with a service). Once a service provider has been located in the registry, a client can then connect to, and interact with, the service based on the services' WSDL document (the UDDI also stores the web address for the WSDL document)[2].

The WSDL is an XML vocabulary standard for Web Services. It allows developers to describe web services and their capabilities in a standard manner. The WSDL helps to expose the web services of various businesses for public access.   Generally speaking, programmers develop services based on their language of choice, while supporting software utilities generally provide the necessary conversions to automatically generate the underlying WSDL document. A WSDL document contains information about a web service and the operations supported by the specific service. A web service

---

[2] It should be noted that UDDI version 3.0 is expected to be extensible in both the UDDI data structures as well as Application Programming Interface (API). So, for example, it will be possible to store a much richer set of service attributes in the UDDI registry as well as access those attributes using the subsequent API. This may make it easier to store the additional attributes associated with OWL-S.

may support multiple operations that can be invoked on that service. Each operation is described in terms of the inputs required by the operation, the outputs generated by the operation as well as the data types for both input and output. Furthermore, the bindings (describing the message format and protocols) are included in the WSDL description.

The SOAP is an XML vocabulary standard to enable programs on separate computers to interact across any network. It is a simple markup language for describing messages between applications. The SOAP provides a way for developers to integrate applications and business processes across the Web or an intranet, by providing the platform and programming language independence needed to create the business integration of web services. A SOAP message contains an *envelope*, *header* and *body* element. The *envelope* element is the root element of a SOAP message. This element defines the XML document as a SOAP message, the namespaces used in the SOAP document as well as the type of encoding (e.g. the data types used in the document). The optional *header* element contains application specific information about the SOAP message. For example, this element is used to describe whether the receiver of the SOAP message must be capable of understanding any number of elements to be communicated in the transaction. The *body* element contains the message.

Figure 6-1 describes the interaction between UDDI, WSDL and SOAP. A service provider registers the necessary service attributes with a UDDI registry including the location of the WSDL document. The client will then look-up the organizations registered within UDDI and the services they have agreed to provide. If a client chooses to use a specific service provided by an organization, that client will then access the services' WSDL document in order to understand how to access the operations available from that service. The communication between the client, UDDI and web service is via SOAP.

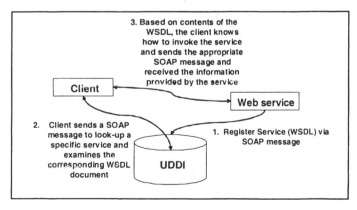

Figure 6-1. Interaction between UDDI, WSDL and SOAP

2.1   Web Service Composition and Semantics

Web service languages that support the specification of service composition and semantics are also emerging, and these have a complementary role to WSDL. These languages provide constructs to enable service composition (e.g., the ability to create services with complex behaviors by linking together other services) as well as the semantic tagging of services. The BPEL specification supports service compositions while the OWL-S goes beyond the features offered by BPEL by providing additional constructs for specifying service semantics. The BPEL language is being developed under the auspices of the OASIS, and its potential benefit is that it enables service reusability. The OWL-S is being advanced under W3C, and its potential benefit is that it promotes a more intelligent mechanism for discovery of services.

The BPEL specification is positioned to become the web service standard for composition. The BPEL defines a business process that specifies the execution of web service operations from a set of web services, the data shared between the operations, the partners involved and also includes various exception handling mechanisms. It permits the specification of complex services by wiring together different activities that can, for example, perform web service invocations, manipulate data, throw faults, or terminate processes. These activities may be nested within structured activities that define how they may be run (e.g., sequence, or in parallel). A conceptual view of BPEL is seen in Figure 6-2 [37]. The BPEL derives its features from Web Services Flow Language [35] and XLANG [36], from IBM and Microsoft respectively.

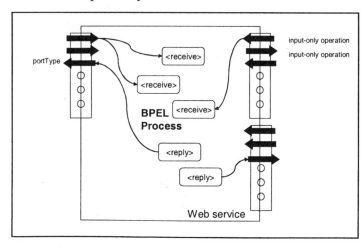

Figure 6-2. Business Process Execution Language (BPEL)

The OWL-S is an example of a semantic web service language [2] and has evolved from the research sponsored by the Defense Advanced Research Projects Agency (DARPA) [7]. Specifically, OWL-S has evolved from the DARPA Agent Markup Language (DAML) [6] and DAML-Services (DAML-S).

The goal of the DAML program (and ontology by the same name) was to develop an XML-based language that describes semantic content to a degree that allows agents to intelligently reason about that content. Traditional markup languages such as the Hyper-Text Markup Language, HTML [16], and the eXtensible Markup Language, XML [10], do not provide sufficient constructs to describe the semantics of information to support intelligent reasoning, being primarily delegated for human consumption. The DAML language leverages concepts found in the Resource Description Framework (RDF) [26] and RDF Schema [27]. The DAML-S was an extension to DAML with the goal of describing semantic content associated with services. The responsibility for evolving the DAML and DAML-S language was eventually given to the W3C, and initial versions have been released under OWL and OWL-S, respectively.

The OWL-S language is described through an ontology that specifies three kinds of knowledge about a service (Figure 6-3). The top level of the OWL-S ontology is the *Service* class, which contains several subclasses. The *ServiceProfile* subclass describes what the service does (e.g., what does the service require of the users and what it provides). This class contains properties that describe the inputs to the service, the output by the service, preconditions that must be valid prior to using the service, and effects the service may have. The *ServiceModel* subclass defines how the service works, and the *ServiceGrounding* subclass specifies how to access the service. Within the *ServiceModel* class there exist constructs for defining atomic services, specifying service compositions as well as for managing flow control (control over how web services are invoked and/or how the information is passed between the services).

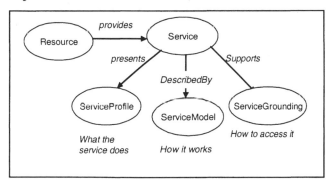

Figure 6-3. Semantic Web Services

2.2   Comparing BPEL, OWL-S and WSDL

The BPEL and OWL-S have broad and somewhat complementary objectives. Both BPEL and OWL-S provide constructs within the language to define complex services in terms of much simpler services, which offers semi-automated processes such as software agents the potential to follow a "recipe' for interacting with such complex services based on the linkages between the underlying services. The *ServiceModel* class within OWL-S most closely relates to the business process model in BPEL, however, the OWL-S enables the semantic tagging of services, which can help a software agent choose between competing services. For example, within OWL-S, one can specify the preconditions that must exist before the service can be used and the effects of using the service. A frequently used example is that if a user is interacting with a book buying service, then a precondition for using this service is that the user must have good credit if purchasing via a credit card. A second key difference between OWL-S and BPEL is that the former is based on a class typing representation that enables reasoning systems to more readily make higher level inferences about the service. The BPEL, on the other hand, does not support such a representation. Business entities that wish to collaborate with each other using BPEL are restricted by structured XML content contained in the WSDL *PortType* definition.

The WSDL does not provide constructs for defining complex services in terms of smaller compositions. However, as BPEL and OWL-S emerge, they may leverage the existing maturity of WSDL, particularly the representation of service bindings. In fact, the *ServiceGrounding* class of OWL-S does not contain a concrete description of service bindings. This OWL-S subclass relies on WSDL for its bindings, as can be seen in Figure 6-4 [38].

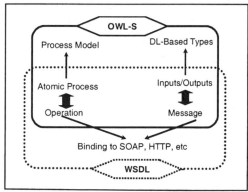

Figure 6-4. Relationship between OWL-S and WSDL

In summary, one of the key differences between OWL-S and BPEL is that OWL-S *ServiceProfile* class provides a much richer set of expressions to support a more intelligent mechanism to interact with a complex service (i.e., inputs, outputs, preconditions and effects). In addition, OWL-S provides the required semantics in order to reason about a service (e.g., based on Description Logic, or DL). The key similarity between OWL-S and BPEL is that both rely to some degree on WSDL. The OWL-S uses the bindings in WSDL to relate the service to a concrete implementation, and BPEL also uses the WSDL specification for its bindings.

The (semantic) web service languages described in this subsection have the potential to empower applications and agents in the GIG to effectively search and utilize services offered by network-centric entities.

3.   THE GLOBAL INFORMATION GRID

The DoD is beginning to invest in the transition of architectures such as the Defense Information Infrastructure (DII) Common Operating Environment (COE) to the Global Information Grid (GIG), which is being managed by the Defense Information Systems Agency.

The vision of the GIG is to provide a truly open environment in which net-centric entities such as Command, Control, Communications, Computers and Intelligence (C4I) systems, simulations, sensors, platforms, software agents, etc., can share information in a seamless manner, without the restrictions and limitations imposed by the DII COE architecture, including a requirement placed on system developers to build within a "closed", but interoperable, environment. This limits interoperability across domains, particularly in a dynamic environment in which opportunistic information is readily available, but may not be easily discovered and accessed.

The GIG represents a fundamental shift from these *stovepiped* architectures to a more open architecture, through the reliance on web-based standards and technologies that enable syntactic interoperability. However, syntactic interoperability alone is not by itself sufficient for meaningful information exchange. In order to achieve meaningful interoperability, one must also consider the information from a contextual perspective in order to achieve semantic interoperability. Semantic web services described in the previous section may provide useful capabilities in this regard.

Another fundamental shift within the GIG vision is from a *"process-then-post"* towards a *"post-then-process"* philosophy, whereby an application will be responsible for fusing and converting raw data or information into a form which is most useful for that particular application. For example, rather than one application requesting information that has been processed by a second application, which does not necessarily know the potential uses of that processed information, the GIG vision allows the first application to find the raw data that is most relevant and do that processing locally so that any intermediate information is not lost.

The GIG architectural model is composed of several layers as seen in Figure 6-5. The lowest layer deals with management and administrative functions such as doctrine, governance, policy, standards and architectures. The next layer above this is the transport, which includes the Defense Information Systems Network [14], Joint Tactical Radio System [17] and Transformation Communication Systems and technology. The purpose of this layer is to physically transport information within the GIG. The next layer above this is the GIG Enterprise Services (ES). The GIG ES layer is comprised of the Core Enterprise Services (CES) and Community of Interest (COI) services. The CES will include basic services that will be required by most components, such as discovery services, storage services, etc. The COI services represent those services that are most useful for a specific group of people or applications. The next layer in the hierarchy are the applications that will interact with the lower level services in order to obtain information necessary for the useful functioning of those applications. The topmost layer is comprised of various war-fighting domains that the applications support.

There are several programs with the DoD that are beginning to implement prototype GIG components. The Net-centric Enterprise Services (NCES) [20] Program, for example, addresses the development of the GIG CES while the Horizontal Fusion initiative [15] addresses the means/tools to support the interaction with the GIG services.

Domains	Examples: •Warfighting •Business •Intelligence
Applications	Examples: •Deployable Joint C2 Program •Business Management Modernization Program
GIG Enterprise Services	Examples: •Electronic Mail •Application Hosting •Weapon-Target Pairing
Transport	Examples: •Defense Information System Network •Joint Tactical Radio System •Transformational Communication System
Management	Examples: •Doctrine •Standards •Governance •Architecture •Policy •Engineering

Figure 6-5. The Global Information Grid (GIG)

Web services technology is expected to provide the underlying mechanism through which information will be shared between the GIG layers. At the time of this writing, the key web technologies envisioned to become a reality in the GIG include UDDI, WSDL and SOAP and to some degree BPEL as they are the most mature technologies. There will be an obvious requirement for users within the GIG to discover and interact with services (whether these be single services or composed of smaller services). However, the WSDL specification does not support the description of semantic relationships, thereby placing a heavy burden on the user/application to determine the appropriateness of the web service for a given usage. Languages such as OWL-S have the potential to make a significant impact to support the intelligent discovery and subsequent interaction with web services by automated software agents. The software agents can interact with an inference engine that has been loaded with the OWL-S ontology, to reason about specific instances corresponding to the ontology.

4.   GIG PROTOTYPE

For years, simulations have been used by analysis and planning staffs to develop and rehearse operation plans, analyze results, and develop doctrine. Typically, combat simulations are used most heavily during the planning stages of an operation, prior to battlefield action. However, simulations are increasingly being used *during* operations to perform CoAA (see description in box below) and develop real-time forecasts of future conditions on the battlefield. Recent efforts by the Defense Modeling and Simulation Office (DMSO) to improve the interoperability of C4I systems with simulations has provided a powerful means for rapid simulation initialization and analysis during exercises, and made simulations more useful and responsive as the exercises are executed. The latest DMSO effort involves technology development to support the integration of operational systems, such as those in the Global Command and Control System (GCCS), with simulations such as the Joint Warfare System (JWARS) [21].

Course of Action (COA) [22]:   (1) A plan that would accomplish, or is related to, the accomplishment of a mission. (2) The scheme adopted to accomplish a mission or task. It is a product of the Joint Operation Planning and Execution System concept development phase.

(Continued from previous page) The recommended course of action will include the concept of operations, evaluation of supportability estimates of supporting organizations, and an integrated time-phased database of combat, combat support and combat service support forces and sustainment. Refinement of this database will be contingent on the time available for course of action development. When approved, the course of action becomes the basis for the development of an operational plan or operational order.

The GCCS [12] is an automated information system designed to support situational awareness and deliberate and crisis planning through the use of an integrated set of analytic tools and flexible data transfer capabilities. GCCS incorporates the force planning and readiness assessment applications required by battlefield commanders to effectively plan and execute military operations. The GCCS system correlates and fuses data from multiple sensors and intelligence sources to provide warfighters the situational awareness needed to be able to act and react decisively. This situational awareness is represented in the Common Operational Picture. It also provides an extensive suite of integrated office automation, messaging, and collaborative applications

The Joint Warfare System (JWARS) [18] is a campaign-level model of military operations that is currently being developed under contract by the U.S. Office of the Secretary of Defense (OSD) for use by OSD, the Joint Staff, the Services, and the Warfighting Commands. JWARS provides users with a representation of joint warfare to support operational planning and execution, force assessment studies, systems effectiveness and trade-off analyses, as well as concept and doctrine development. The JWARS permits studies that require a "balanced representation of Joint Warfare", with models that support 1) the C4ISR systems and processes that are an integral part of US concept of operations; 2) logistics, both strategic and intra-theater in the combat area; and 3) maneuver warfare at the operational level.

The DMSO is sponsoring the integration of JWARS, GCCS and software agents as a proof-of-principle to demonstrate the viability of supporting the interoperability of these three components through the application of web service technologies, Figure 6-6.

4.1 Concept of Operations

The concept of operations of this proof-of-principle evaluation is to initialize GCCS with Unit Order of Battle (UOB) data to represent known locations of forces prior to plan execution. The JWARS is also initialized with the same UOB data to ensure that it is consistent with the force structure in GCCS. Through an artificial mechanism, the GCCS will generate real-time updates to track movements. The reason for the artificial generation of track movements is due to the fact that the demonstration is in a laboratory environment, and hence the system is not integrated with live information feeds; however, this is an assumption that does not invalidate the concept or the application of the technology. The JWARS simulation is capable of generating "expected" movement of the same forces based on its internal models and algorithms.

Both the actual GCCS track data as well as the corresponding JWARS expected track movements will be made available to the software agents, which will compare such things as deviations between real/expected track positions, whether certain tracks enter regions of interest (or, alternatively, fail to do so) in a given time period or time instant, actual versus expected force ratios, etc. The failure conditions, as specified by the user, will trigger the agents to send alerts to both GCCS and JWARS, after which JWARS can be used to spawn additional JWARS simulations to support CoAA in order to correct the failures in the plan.

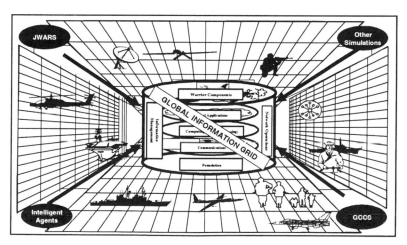

Figure 6-6. JWARS and GCCS interoperability with Intelligent Agents in the GIG

The proof-of-principle demonstration will utilize tracks associated with units (e.g. land and sea) from the GCCS Track Management Server (TMS) as well as air tracks coming from the Theatre Battle Management Core

System (TBMCS). These tracks will be made available to the agents through web service technology.

4.2   System Operation

The basic architecture supporting the proof-of-principle integration between JWARS, GCCS and software agents is seen in Figure 6-7. This architecture leverages the web service technologies UDDI, WSDL and SOAP to enable the syntactic interoperability between each component.

The Army C4I Simulation Initialization System [3] is used to initialize the GCCS-M TMS and TBMCS [31] C4I systems as well as the simulation system (i.e., JWARS). The initialization information contains the current UOB such as organizations, their command relationships, as well as supporting equipment and facilities. A tactical system (in our case, an exercise replay) will deliver the actual data to GCCS.

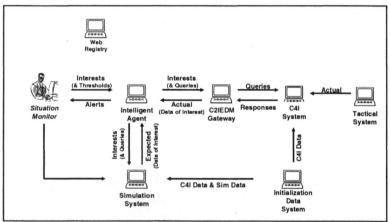

Figure 6-7. The JWARS, GCCS and Software Agent Web Service Federation

The Situation Monitor (SM) is a graphical front end which permits a JWARS user to specify tracks of interest that need to be monitored, and any conditions and corresponding thresholds to which the user would like to be alerted when these conditions are met or thresholds are exceeded. The SM invokes the *subscribeFor* operation of the *TrackMonitorWebService,* in order to send the intelligent agents behind this service the subsequent tracks that the user has an interest in monitoring for deviation analysis.

A small fragment of this web service's XSD file is contained in Table 6-1 and WSDL file is contained in Table 6-2. As can be seen from the WSDL, this operation contains a *subscribeFor* input message and *subscribeForResponse* output message. The input message corresponds to a *TrackRegistration* object described in the corresponding XSD file. The object consists of a list of track identification numbers, criteria for generating alerts and thresholds to be used to detect deviations as received by the web service. This information will be communicated to software agents that will make requests to the C4I system and simulation to obtain the corresponding tracks for subsequent monitoring. The software agents receive the tracks after invoking both the *C2IEDMGatewayService* as well as the *JWARSWebService* (the data from *C4ISystemTrackService* is translated to the C2IEDM interchange format – discussed later – by the *C2IEDMGatewayService*). These agents will compare both the real and simulated tracks using the thresholds to generate alerts, which are sent back to the SM display (again, through the invocation of operations corresponding to the *SituationMonitorWebService*.) The alerts may warrant the exploration of "what-ifs" in order to aid in the analysis and selection of alternative courses of action.

Table 6-1. TrackMonitorWebService XSD (XML Schema Document)

```
***
<xsd:complexType name="TrackRegistration" >
    <xsd:annotation>
***
</xsd:annotation>
  <xsd:sequence>
      <xsd:element minOccurs="1" maxOccurs="1"
          name="wsName" type="xsd:string"/>
    <xsd:element minOccurs="1" maxOccurs="unbounded"
        name="trackIds" type="xsd:string"/>
    <xsd:element minOccurs="0" maxOccurs="unbounded"
        name="criteria" type="xsd:string"/>
    <xsd:element minOccurs="0" maxOccurs="unbounded"
        name="thresholds" type="xsd:string"/>
  </xsd:sequence>
  </xsd:complexType>
***
```

Table 6-2. TrackMonitorWebService WSDL

```
<types>
    <xsd:schema targetNamespace=
            "http://www.TrackMonitorWebService.com/
                TrackMonitorWebService/xsd"
        xmlns:xsd="http://www.w3.org/2001/XMLSchema">
    <xsd
ttp://www.TrackMonitorWebService.com/
                TrackMonitorWebService/xsd"
        schemaLocation="TrackMonitorWebService.xsd"/>
    </xsd:schema>
<xsd:element name="subscribeFor"
            type="trackMonitorSchema:TrackRegistration"/>
***
</xsd:schema>
</types>
  <message name="subscribeFor">
    <part name="body" element="tmws:subscribeFor"/>
***
<operation name="subscribeFor">
        <input message="tns:subscribeFor"/>
        <output message="tns:subscribeForResponse"/>
</operation>
***
```

Each of the services in Figure 6-7 will register themselves with the UDDI registry. Each component will then do a look-up within UDDI to obtain the WSDL file of the other services, from which the service can dynamically resolve the location of the other services, and subsequently invoke their operations.

The Command and Control Information Exchange Data Model (C2IEDM) [4] gateway will map the information passed between services onto the C2IEDM vocabulary. The C2IEDM was developed under the auspices of the Multilateral Interoperability Programme.

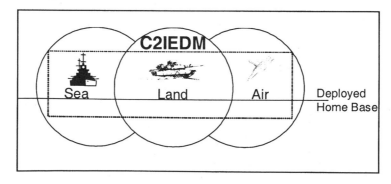

Figure 6-8. The scope of the C2IEDM data model

The C2IEDM is a generic model that can be extended as needed to suit evolving military requirements (e.g., serves as a "hub"; as such, it was originally named the "Generic Hub", and evolved to Land C2IEDM and eventually C2IEDM to capture other areas including Air and Surface, see Figure 6-8). The C2IEDM is comprised of a conceptual data model, logical data model and physical data model. The conceptual data model represents generalized concepts, while the logical data model represents further details associated with the conceptual data model. The physical data model defines the physical data storage schema. The main purpose of the C2IEDM is to represent Information Exchange Requirements between C2 systems.

The proof-of-principle prototype is currently undergoing experimentation in a laboratory environment and, through feedback from subject matter experts, the capability will be refined. We expect to provide these unique CoAA services to the broader GIG community through participation in integrated experiments in the future.

5.   CHALLENGES FOR AGENTS IN THE GIG

There are many challenges in realizing such an ambitious effort as the GIG. One challenge we are faced with in our proof-of-principle implementation is the integration of large legacy systems through web services, which, although maturing at a fast pace, are still evolving. This, by itself, is a tremendous challenge as we are forced to reengineer legacy software to work within a different computing paradigm (the standards for which are continually evolving)! It is envisioned that newer systems in the GIG will be architected to seamlessly work with web services technology.

Having an ability to semi-automatically locate and interact with services will be a key capability, as it will be inefficient to have users in the loop on every transaction to search for web services. Furthermore, systems and components in the GIG may lack the time to form complex search queries. We envision intelligent agents to support this functionality through their abilities to semi-autonomously coordinate with other agents and humans in support of system requirements for information.

Another issue that will inevitably be encountered in the GIG will include the interoperability of systems between Communities of Interest (COI). For example, the Modeling and Simulation COI may rely upon the C2IEDM as the common information exchange model, but this may not be appropriate or adopted for use throughout the GIG. The challenge here will be to develop techniques that map/translate between meta-data or ontologies that are expected to exist across the many COIs. What will be the role of agents in supporting this process, or will this be primarily a manual process?

A key challenge that is certain to arise will be the ability of agents (which understand one ontology) to communicate with other agents (having a different ontological representations). Again, technologies that aid in mapping or translating between ontologies will support the ability of agents to communicate within the GIG environment, which may lead to coordinated agent activity. The field of agent coordination and teamwork is an emerging area of research [25, 30]. To realize the full potential of distributed multi-agent systems, the agents will need to cooperate as part of teams to help the operators (i.e., acting as their proxies) achieve their goals. In the context of our proof-of-principle, teams of distributed software agents with different goals and ontologies may need to coordinate to decompose and relate multiple plans to determine critical points, which may be communicated to a team of agents responsible for monitoring the critical points in the plan's execution.

In the GIG, agents may be required to assess the viability of dynamically composing a service; therefore, it may be necessary to endow these agents with advanced reasoning capabilities. However, there will be a limit in terms of how much an agent is able to practically reason with, hence, additional solutions may be adopted. The additional techniques may include human-agent cooperation (i.e., mixed-initiative approaches), potentially coupled with machine learning techniques in order to create robust, adaptive agents.

6.   POTENTIAL LIMITATION OF WEB SERVICES FOR THE GIG

There are several challenges in applying web service technologies in a network-centric environment such as the GIG. The web-service computing paradigm was primarily developed to support Business-to-Business (B2B) commerce in which services offered by businesses could be invoked using web technology. Of course, there are still open questions in using web services in a B2B computing world, such as, for example, payment for services rendered. As the commercial sector is primarily driving the development of web service technology, any solution generated from the commercial sector may have the potential to be used in some form within the military domain. A bigger question, however, concerns reliability. For example, in B2B commerce, it may be acceptable for services to fail quite often, for example, if a service is being upgraded or a computer system goes down. A high level of failure may not be acceptable in a military environment in which the lives of humans may potentially be at stake. How will Quality of Service be guaranteed, what criteria will be used and under what circumstances? This may imply a tight coupling between the upper layers and the lower layers in the GIG.

Another question regarding the use of web services is "how well is the technology suited to the potential bottlenecks associated with the registries?" After all, the client application must know the location of the registries in order to be able to access them and determine what services have been registered and how to access them. What should happen if the nodes that the registries reside on fail, or are bombarded with a potential denial of service attack? Possibly a larger issue to consider is "how will highly mobile platforms and systems interact with registries?" These platforms operate at a very high tempo and connectivity to such registries may be sporadic.

Agent technology has the potential to make a profound impact within the GIG; however, one must also consider whether web services will provide the necessary infrastructure for agent-to-agent coordination. For example, agents may be required to coordinate with each other through bi-directional messaging. This, however, may not be adequately supported through a web services framework. For example, communication between agents does not necessarily fit within the SOA paradigm; an agent's communications capability should not necessarily be categorized as a service that is provided by that agent. Instead, the agents should be able to communicate through a natural metaphor, utilizing web services as needed to perform their functions.

It is apparent that web services will enable much of the interoperability in the GIG, but may not be the silver bullet solution for every situation. Can we assume that web services will be sufficiently mature in the future to address these issues? There is certainly a possibility that web services may not be the only solution, but may be required to work with a variety of supporting technologies that offer a solution to these limitations (a quick look through W3C's activity reveals a heterogeneous mix of technologies being developed which offer varying capabilities suitable for different uses).

7.   SURVEY OF COMPETING TECHNOLOGIES

The field of grid computing may be considered a subcategory of distributed computing [11], and may complement web services. There is a subtle difference between grid computing and distributed computing. Generally speaking, the world of grid computing deals with the *large-scale* sharing or utilization of loosely coupled, distributed, heterogeneous resources. Distributed computing, on the other hand, primarily deals with allocating software components on a smaller scale across a network (e.g., to conserve computation cycles on a local machine.)   Grid computing holds the promise of taking distributed computing to a new level that enables computing across the internet.

Grid computing, and to some degree distributed computing, may be further characterized as either client-server or Peer-to-Peer (P2P) [23]. Web services technology is most closely related to the client-server model. For example, UDDI registries store information regarding available services, and clients access those registries to determine where the service resides and how to access it.

In a P2P computing environment, there are no centralized registries; a subset of the directory peers maintain a local cache of available service advertisements of peers that choose to register with that particular directory. Any peer requiring a service may dynamically discover and interact with these directories to locate a service offered by other peers. In fact, in a P2P infrastructure, peers are generally dynamically discovered through the interaction with directories that maintain service advertisements. These advertisements allow peers to discover and utilize the services of other peers.

Although the P2P computing landscape is large, the next two subsections will present representative examples of P2P systems. Project JXTA captures some of the primary characteristics of P2P systems, while Neurogrid provides a flavor of intelligent search and discovery in P2P environments. The third subsection will describe the Control of Agent Based Systems (CoABS) Grid. The CoABS grid is not considered a pure P2P system, but is more closely aligned with a client-server model.   The CoABS grid is presented because it has been used extensively by the software agent community to federate agent-based systems.

7.1   Project JXTA

Project JXTA [24] is an implementation of P2P computing that is being advocated by Sun Microsystems. JXTA provides an open set of XML-based protocols that allows any device on a given network to communicate and collaborate in a P2P fashion, even when some of the peers are behind Network Attached Devices or Firewalls.   The basic concepts supported by JXTA are the *peer*, *peer group*, *network services*, *modules*, *pipes*, *messages*, and *advertisements* which are described below:

- *Peer:* A peer in JXTA is any device on the network that supports one or more of the JXTA protocols.   There are six protocols defined within JXTA. Peers use these protocols to discover other peers, advertise and discover network resources, as well as communicate and route messages.

- *Peer Group:* A peer group is a collection of peers that have an agreed upon set of services. Peers may exist within multiple peer groups simultaneously; however, by default, when peers are instantiated they are joined to the Net Peer Group (all peers are a part of the Net Peer Group).
- *Network Services:* Peers generally cooperate and communicate to discover network services. There are two types of services: *Peer services* and *Peer Group Services.* The former type of service is associated with an individual peer while the latter service type is associated with a group of peers, which provides the added advantage of redundancy among the peers in the group (assuming another peer is still able to provide the failed service).
- *Modules:* Modules are pieces of code written to represent any kind of behavior, and are described by the *Module Class* (which supports the capability to advertise behaviors), *Module Specification* (which provides support to access a module) and *Module Implementation* (the actual implementation of the module). Network services are the most common forms of behavior that can be instantiated on a peer.
- *Pipes:* Pipes support communication between peers. Input pipes are used by peers to receive messages; output pipes are used to send messages.
- *Messages:* A message is an object that is transmitted between JXTA peers. Messages may be either in XML or binary form.
- *Advertisements:* Advertisements are XML documents that describe peers, peer groups, pipes or services. There are nine advertisement types that are supported in JXTA.

Using the JXTA architecture, peers advertise their capabilities with a rendezvous peer (i.e., directory), which caches the advertisement. The advertisement may include the service offered as well as information about how to connect to the peer that offers the service. If a peer wishes to discover a service, and an advertisement is not found on the local rendezvous peer, then a discovery request is propagated by that rendezvous peer to other rendezvous peers on the network. A rendezvous peer that contains the specific service advertisement provides the pipe advertisement to the requesting peer, which uses the pipe advertisements to connect directly with the peer that offers the service.

Relay peers contain routes to other peers, and are also capable of routing messages to peers. In the example above, if the service is not found on the local rendezvous peer, then a route is needed to other rendezvous peers as well as eventually to the peer that offers a service. The route will be contained as a series of hops through a set of relay peers to the destination. Rendezvous and relay peers may be implemented on the same node.

7.2   NeuroGrid

The Neurogrid [19] environment provides a decentralized, adaptive search system that learns over time in response to user queries. Two main components of Neurogrid that complement one another are semantic routing and learning. Semantic routing refers to the ability to forward queries based on their content, while learning in this context refers to the ability of the nodes to dynamically adjust the meta-data describing the contents of nodes and the files that make up those contents.

The concept behind NeuroGrid is to store the relationship between bookmarked URL's and their relationships to user queries (e.g., keywords) as well as between keywords and other nodes, which then provides a capability to semantically route discovery requests between nodes in order to determine which nodes offer the best response (e.g, URL) to the query (keywords, or metadata, may also be updated at this point). A direct link is also formed between the initiating node as well as the node that returns the response, thereby increasing the connectivity in the network. Neurogrid addresses the issue of how to rank multiple URLs that are associated with the same keyword by not only using the fact that the user has clicked through the URL, but whether it was bookmarked as well. The mathematics behind Neurogrid also takes into account cases where the ratio of recommended bookmarks to that of selected bookmarks, for a given search, is identical.

NeuroGrid, in its current server side implementation is not a pure P2P system in the sense that each node is connected to every other node. It is, however, based around a large number of small servers being linked to one another in a P2P fashion, with each server supporting a small community of users

7.3   The CoABS Grid

The CoABS grid [5] (hereafter referred to as Grid) was developed under the DARPA CoABS program, and arguably provides the most successful and widely used infrastructure to date for the large-scale integration of heterogeneous agent frameworks with object-based applications, and legacy systems. Based on Sun's Jini [29] services, it includes a method-based application-programming interface to register and advertise capabilities, discovers services based on those capabilities, and provides the necessary communication between services. Systems and components on the Grid can be added and upgraded without reconfiguration of the network. Failed or unavailable components are automatically purged from the registry and discovery of similar services and functionality is pursued.

The Grid supports a wide variety of applications, from those that support simple monitoring and information retrieval to complex, dynamic domains such as military command and control. Using the Grid, agents and wrapped legacy systems can (1) describe their needs, capabilities and interfaces to other agents and legacy systems; (2) find and work with other agent components and legacy systems to accomplish complex tasks in flexible teams; (3) interact with humans and other agents to accept tasking and present results, and (4) adapt to changes in the application domain, the task at hand, or the computing environment. The Grid does this by providing access to shared policies and ontologies (mechanisms for describing agents' capabilities and needs), and services that support interoperability among agents and legacy systems with simple or rich levels of semantics—all distributed across a network infrastructure.

Although most agent frameworks provide some of the interoperability and other services that the Grid provides, each framework typically supports specialized constructs, communication, and control mechanisms. This specialization is desirable because particular systems can use mechanisms appropriate to the problem domain/task to be solved. The Grid is not intended to replace current agent frameworks but rather to augment their capabilities with services supporting trans-architecture teams.

The Grid provides helper utility classes that are local to an agent and hide the complexity of Jini. These classes automatically find any Look-up Services in both the local area network and user-designated distant machines. The Grid supports agent and service discovery based on Jini entries and arbitrary predicates as well as by service type. The Grid also provides event notification when agents register, deregister, or change their advertised attributes.

Recently DARPA has conceived a new program within the Information Processing Technology Office (IPTO) called Fast Connectivity for Coalition and Agents Project (FastC2AP). One of the goals of the FastC2AP program is to investigate and build linkages between the CoABS grid and web services. The idea is to make web services easily accessible to software agents on the grid. Programs such as this demonstrate that web service technology is maturing fast and permeating into military applications. However, it is becoming apparent that architectures more suited to large-scale multi-agent systems, such as the CoABS grid, will continue to be used and will therefore be required to work with web services.

8.   SUMMARY

This chapter has described the current state-of-the-art in web services technology and how it is being applied to support the development of the GIG. This chapter has also described a proof-of-principle implementation that uses web services to support the interoperability between a military system, simulation and intelligent agents to support CoAA. Future areas to explore in the proof-of-principle include the integration with the eXtensible Battle Management Language [32], which enables access to military Operational Orders (OPORDS) through a web service interface. This will enable the agents to relate the impact of the deviations to the OPORD (particularly whether critical tasks within the OPORD are affected by the deviations). Additional areas include the use of BPEL to configure services from within the JWARS Situation Monitor and exploring techniques for mapping between ontologies to support agent-to-agent communication.

This chapter has also outlined the challenging problems that software agents may be expected to not only face, but also help solve in the GIG. The issues that have been suggested include:

- The integration of agent technology within a web-services paradigm.
- Interoperability of systems between the GIG COI's and whether software agents (which understand one ontology) will be able to effectively (e.g., semantically) communicate with other agents (having a different ontological representation).
- Limitations associated with the reasoning capabilities of software agents in the GIG, and whether human-agent cooperation will be necessary and can agents learn from this interaction?

Lastly, this chapter has outlined the potential limitations of web service technology to support the full operational concept of the GIG, and discussed the role of competing architectures such as JXTA, Neurogrid and CoABS grid. It is unclear how web service technology will evolve to meet the needs of the GIG. For example, industry watchers now proclaim the next big revolution to be grid services, which offers a mechanism to enable, among other things, reliability in accessing services through new WSDL specifications. The continuing evolution of web services and related technology will certainly impact the deployment of software agent technology in the GIG. The big question is *"will there be a single technology that provides the infrastructure for the GIG, or will there be several complementary technologies that also provide better support for software agents?"* If the latter is true, questions of how to best bridge the applications that rely on different technologies will need to be answered?

9. REFERENCES

1. Ankolekar, M. Burstein, J. Hobbs, O. Lassila, D. Martin, S. McIlraith, S. Narayanan, M. Paolucci, T. Payne, K. Sycara, H. Zeng, "DAML-S: Semantic Markup for Web Services", In *Proceedings of the International Semantic Web Working Symposium (SWWS)*, July 30-August 1, 2001
2. Berners-Lee, T. Hendler, J. Lassila, Ora. (2001). The Semantic Web. *Scientific American.* 279(5), pp. 35-43 (2001).
3. Carlton, B. Scrudder, R. Black, C. Hopkins, M. Initialization of C4I Systems and Simulation Federations – Today and in the Future, In *Proceedings of the 2004 Fall Simulation Interoperability Workshop* (2004)
4. C2IEDM, http://www.mip-site.org
5. Control of Agent Based System Grid, http://coabs.globalinfotek.com
6. DARPA Agent Markup Language, http://www.daml.org
7. Defense Advanced Research Projects Agency, http://www.darpa.mil
8. Defense Information Infrastructure (DII) Common Operating Environment (COE), http://diicoe.disa.mil/coe
9. ebXML Web Site, http://www.ebxml.org
10. eXtensible Markup Language, http://www.w3.org/XML/
11. Foster, I. Kesselman, K. Tuecke, S. The Anatomy of a Grid: Enabling Scalable Virtual Organizations. *International Journal of Supercomputer Applications*, 15(3), pp. 200-222, Fall 2001.
12. Global Command and Control System Common Operational Picture Reporting Requirements, CJCSI 3151-01A (19th January 2003)
13. Global Information Grid (GIG), http://ges.dod.mil, http://www.disa.mil/ns/gig.html
14. Hawkins, J. Defense Information Systems Network (DISN): Policy, Responsibilities and Processes. July 2003, http://www.dtic.mil/cjcs_directives/cdata/unlimit/6211_02.pdf
15. Horizontal Fusion, http://horizontalfusion.dod.mil
16. Hypertext Markup Language, http://www.w3.org/MarkUp/
17. Joint Tactical Radio System, http://jtrs.army.mil
18. Joint Warfare Simulation, http://www.caci.com/business/systems/simulation/jwars.shtml
19. Joseph S. (2002) "NeuroGrid: Semantically Routing Queries in Peer-to-Peer Networks." In *Proceedings of the International Workshop on Peer-to-Peer Computing* (co-located with Networking 2002), Pisa, Italy, May 2002.
20. Meyerriecks, D. Net-Centric Enterprise Services. *Military Information Technology Online Archives,* **7** (3), 2003.
21. Mittu, R., Walters, J., Abramson, M., "Improving Simulation Analysis through Interfaces to C4I systems and Simulations", In *Proceedings of the 2004 Spring Simulation Interoperability Workshop.*, Crystal City, VA.
22. Naval Doctrine Command. *Naval Doctrine Publication 5: Naval Planning.* 1996
23. Peer-to-Peer Computing, http://www.openp2p.com
24. Project JXTA Web site, http://www.jxta.org
25. Rao A. S. and Georgeff M. P. "BDI agents: from Theory to Practice". In *Proceedings of the First Intl. Conference on Multiagent Systems*, San Francisco, 1995.
26. Resource Description Framework, http://www.w3c.org/RDF/
27. Resource Description Framework Schema, http://www.w3.org/TR/rdf-schema/
28. Sherman, Doron. BPEL Unleashed: Putting a Modern Business Process Execution Standard to Work. *Web Services Journal,* **5** (1), pp. 18, 34-36.
29. Sun Microsystems, Jini Network Technology: An Executive Overview, http://wwws.sun.com/software/jini/whitepapers/jini-execoverview.pdf

30. Tambe, M. "Agent Architectures for Flexible, Practical Teamwork". In *Proceedings of the National Conference on Artificial Intelligence*, 1997.
31. Theatre Battle Management Core System, http://www.fas.org/man/dod-101/sys/ac/equip/tbmcs.htm
32. Tolk, Andreas, Pullen, J. Mark, Sudnikovich, W. Hieb, M. "Developing Battle Management Language into a Web Service". In *Proceedings of 2004 Spring Simulation Interoperability Workshop*. Crystal City, VA.
33. Wooldridge, M. *An Introduction to MultiAgent Systems*, John Wiley and Sons, 2002.
34. World Wide Web Consortium (W3C), http://www.w3c.org
35. WSFL: http://xml.coverpages.org/wsfl.html
36. XLANG: http://xml.coverpages.org/xlang.html
37. http://www-106.ibm.com/developerworks/webservices/library/ws-bpelcol1/
38. DAML Services Coalition (alphabetically A. Ankolekar, M. Burstein, J. Hobbs, O. Lassila, D. Martin, S. McIlraith, S. Narayanan, M. Paolucci, T. Payne, K. Sycara, H. Zeng), "DAML-S: Semantic Markup for Web Services",*Proceedings of the International Semantic Web Working Symposium* (SWWS), July 30-August 1, 2001

Chapter 7

A MULTI-AGENT ARCHITECTURE FOR DISTRIBUTED DOMAIN-SPECIFIC INFORMATION INTEGRATION

Shahram Rahimi[1], Norm Carver[1] and Frederick Petry[2]
[1]Department of Computer Science, Southern Illinois University, Carbondale, IL 62901-4511;
[2]Electrical Engineering and Computer Science Dept,Tulane University, New Orleans, LA 70118

Abstract: On both the public Internet and private Intranets, there is a vast amount of data available that is owned and maintained by different organizations, distributed all around the world. These data resources are rich and recent; however, information gathering and knowledge discovery from them, in a particular knowledge domain, confronts major difficulties. The objective of this chapter is to introduce an autonomous methodology to provide for domain-specific information gathering and integration from multiple distributed sources.

Key words: multi-agent systems; information integration; distributed systems; knowledge discovery.

1.   INTRODUCTION AND BACKGROUND

The Internet has drastically changed the availability of electronically accessible information. According to a Cyveillance study released in July 2000 [30], the Internet contains over 2 billion unique, publicly accessible pages which are accessed and updated by millions of users internationally. Automated data collection tools and mature database technology lead to tremendous amounts of data stored in databases, data warehouses and other information repositories. The available data sources include traditional and object oriented databases, knowledge bases, flat files, formatted files (such as XML), vector maps and raster images, videos and audios.

With the growing number of information sources available, the problem of exploiting and integrating distributed and heterogeneous information sources is becoming more and more critical. Information gathering and integration from Internet and Intranet sources faces several challenges. First, the variety and amount of the data sources are increasing dramatically day by day. Second the general information is unorganized, imprecise, of diverse format, and is distributed on several servers through heterogeneous networks all over the world. Third, the availability and reliability of information are changing constantly. Consequently, in large-scale network environments such as the Internet, it is becoming more and more difficult to use the traditional methods to retrieve and integrate information efficiently and even more difficult to perform knowledge discovery.

An effective information integration mechanism should provide the basis for a rich "knowledge space" built on top of the basic Internet "data layer". This knowledge layer should be composed of value-added services that process and offer abstracted information and knowledge, rather than returning documents (in the manner of most current web search engines).

Traditional approaches to building distributed systems do not scale well to the large, diverse and growing number of information sources. Technologies such as *Softbot* [13], Sage [21], Occam [22], *ARACHNID* [29], *Meta search engines* [16], Web Robot, Spider, Clower [17], *WebWatcher* [19], and *ShopBot* [11] provide very few capabilities for locating, combining, processing, organizing, and abstracting information about a specific knowledge domain. For these systems several open problems remain:

• *Gathering pieces of knowledge:* In all conventional systems, the gathered information is only a set of pieces of knowledge. Science and engineering researchers, as well as decision makers, need more systematic and deeply integrated knowledge on a target domain. For instance, decision makers need a system that provides them with real-time developed knowledge, which includes all the necessary components for decision making. For example, if a decision is to be made for an offensive move toward Baghdad, the system should provide the commanders with comprehensive knowledge. The components of the provided knowledge by the system for such a query could include weather, logistics, maps, pictures, positions (enemy/friendly/neutral troops), etc. Moreover, other related information that may help with the decision making process such as "how operational is the enemy's central command system," should be available. Therefore, a simple one line query to the system should gather, process and categorize the related information for the user.

• *Client-Server Approach:* All the above technologies use traditional client-server approach. In this approach the client computer needs to maintain a continuous communication link with the server. This not only causes both computers (the client and the server) to stay busy with their respective processes until the end of the task, but also they have to continually send and receive messages required for the accomplishment of their task. This imposes a considerable amount of traffic on the network. The client-server model has confronted several challenges, such as problematic legacy network, scaling and protocol problems.

Recently, there is a growing interest in using an intelligent agent approach for designing systems that assist users on the WWW. Because of the flexible and dynamic characteristics of intelligent agents, they are being used widely as interface system between the user and the WWW for different applications. For example, Bollacker developed an agent that assists the user on scientific literature search [5], Ackerman an agent that finds web pages for the user [1], and Leberman an agent for helping users to browse the WWW [24]. Other attempts such as [10] have used a multi-agent approach to help users with common interest to share Web pages, or Martin et al. and Hu et al. which have proposed an agent-based brokering facilitation between users and various information resources [27,16]. More recently, work by Lesser and associates on agent-based information gathering resulted in the BIG (resource-Bounded Information Gathering) agent architecture [25]. BIG integrates a number of AI technologies, including a real-time planner and scheduler, a task modeling tool, and an information extraction/understanding component [7,25,14]. The resulting system can reason about resource trade-offs for alternative methods for gathering information, and can potentially use the extracted information to refine its further search and processing activities.

The single-agent approaches are designed to assist users for a specific task. These systems are limited to a particular job and are not scalable enough to be expanded to a general information gathering system (and definitely not an information integration one). On the other hand, today's most advanced multi-agent approaches aim for information gathering in the form of pieces of knowledge. These architectures do not systematically offer developed knowledge on a target domain that includes all the necessary components to fulfill a query. They lack seriously the capability of categorizing available information and providing mechanisms to deal with different data formats on the WWW.

In this chapter an intelligent agent approach to design and implementation issues is described. We are proposing an integrated system that provides access to a large number of information sources, in a particular domain, by organizing them into a network of information agents. Each agent provides expertise on a specific topic by drawing on relevant information from other information agents in related knowledge domains. Every information agent contains an *ontology* of its domain of expertise, its *domain model*, and models of the other agents that can provide relevant information, its *information source models*. Similar to the way current information sources are independently constructed, information agents can be developed and maintained separately. They draw on other information agents and data repositories to provide a new information source that others can build upon in turn. Each information agent is another information source, but provides an *abstraction* of the many information sources available. An existing data repository can be turned into a simple information agent by building the appropriate interface code, called a wrapper, that will allow it to conform to the conventions of the organization. The advantage of using wrappers is that it greatly simplifies the individual agents since they only need to handle one underlying format.

The rest of this chapter is organized as follow. In section 2, the use of intelligent agents as the basic building block of the system is justified. In sections 3 and 4 the architecture of the system is presented and discussed. Finally, section 5 concludes the chapter.

2.   THE BASIC BUILDING BLOCK – INTELLIGENT AGENTS

In order to effectively use the many heterogeneous information sources available in large computer networks, such as the Internet, we need some form of organization. The concept of an agent that provides expertise on a specific topic, by drawing on relevant information from a variety of sources, offers the basic building block.

With the availability of low cost mobile devices, such as mobile PCs and PDAs, people are able to access information available on the fixed network anywhere, anytime (providing sufficient transmitter coverage). This means that for any information providing tool to be operational, it should be capable of supporting mobile devices. In wireless network environments, the mobile devices face several limitations, such as low bandwidth, low computing power, small memory capacity, low battery life, etc., restricting the mobile computing [32]. The advent of mobile agent technology is expected to overcome these limitations. Mobile agents are specialized independent programs executing on behalf of users. They are transported to multiple remote hosts in the network to carry out assigned tasks. Therefore, potentially they can reduce the communication traffic in the network. This makes them attractive for mobile communications and scalable systems.

Moreover, intelligent agents are differentiated from other applications by their added dimensions of autonomy, and the ability to interact independent of its user's presence. These characteristics make intelligent agents an attractive choice to be used in our model for real-time knowledge discovery and integration [32].

3.   NETWORK OF INFORMATION AGENTS

We believe that a promising approach to distributed information integration is to access the large number of information sources by organizing them into a network of *information agents* [20]. The goal of each information agent is to provide information and expertise on a specific topic by drawing on relevant abstracted information from other information agents. To build such a network, we need an appropriate architecture for a single information agent that can be instantiated to provide multiple agents. A proposed architecture [28] has been used with some modifications in our prototype [33,38].

Similar to the way current information sources are independently constructed, information agents are developed and maintained separately. They draw on other information agents and data repositories to provide a new information source that others can build upon in turn. Each information agent is another information source, but provides an abstraction of the many information sources available. An existing information source is turned into a simple information agent by building the appropriate interface code, called a wrapper, that allows it to conform to the conventions of the organization (described below). A class of wrapper agents would need to be built for any given type of information source (e.g., imagery, graphics, text, formatted text, video and audio, etc). The advantage of this approach is that it greatly simplifies the individual agents since they only need to handle one underlying format. This makes it possible to scale the network into many agents with access to many different types of information sources.

In this system, some agents answer queries addressed to them, but do not actively originate requests for information to others; we will refer to these as *data repositories (wrapper agents)*. These agents correspond to different information sources including relational databases, object oriented databases, imagery and graphic sources, vector and raster maps, text and formatted text sources, and audio/video sources. For each one of these categories there is an intelligent agent with adequate expertise for knowledge discovery. In the following, we will use the term *data repository* or *wrapper agent* when we want to emphasize such agents, otherwise we will use the term *information agent*. Data repositories in our model are described in the next section.

Figure 1 shows an example network of information agents that will be used to explain different parts of the system. The application domain is logistics planning. In order to perform its task, the Logistic_Planning_Agent, which is an information agent, needs to obtain information on different topics, such as transportation capabilities, weather conditions and geographic data. The other agents must also integrate a number of sources of information that are relevant to their domain of expertise. For example, the Sea_Agent combines assets data from the Naval_Agent (such as ships from different fleets), harbor data from the Harbor_Agent and the Port_Agent (such as storage space or cranes in harbors, channels, etc; information that has been obtained, in turn, from repositories of different geographical areas).

There are several points to note about this network that relate to the autonomy of the agents. First, each agent may choose to integrate only those parts of the ontologies of its information sources necessary for the task that it is designed for. For example, the Transportation_Agent might have a fairly complete integration of the Sea, Land and Air_agents, while the Logistics_Planning_Agent might draw on only some parts of the knowledge of the Weather and Geographic_agents. Second, we may need to build new agents if we cannot find an existing one that contains all the information needed. For example, if the Geographic_Agent did not include some particular geopolitical facts required by the Logistics_Planning_Agent, the latter could access directly the Geopolitical_information_Agent. However, if much of the information was not represented, an alternative geographic agent would need to be constructed (and linked). Third, the network forms a directed acyclic graph, not a tree, because a particular agent may provide information to several others that focus on different aspects of its expertise (like the Port_Agent that is accessed by the

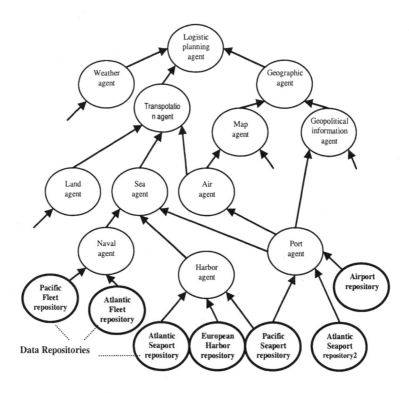

Figure 7-1. Network of information gathering agents

Geopolitical, Air and Sea-agents). Nevertheless, cycles should be avoided; otherwise a query may loop endlessly without finding some agent that can actually answer it.

In summary, the network of information gathering agents provides the basis for a rich "knowledge space" built on top of the basic web "data layer". This knowledge layer is composed of value-added services that process and offer abstracted information and knowledge, rather than returning documents. In spite of the complexity introduced by respecting the autonomy of the agents in the organization, the fact that individual agents can be independently built and maintained makes the system flexible enough to scale to large numbers of information sources and adaptable to the needs of new applications.

4.   THE SYSTEM ARCHITECTURE

The network of information gathering agents is built on an autonomous administrative infrastructure (AAI). For this structure, the initial framework design incorporates the use of mobile request agent (MRA), mobile supporting agent (MSA), user interface agent (UIA), information manager agent (IMA), and agent administrator (AA).

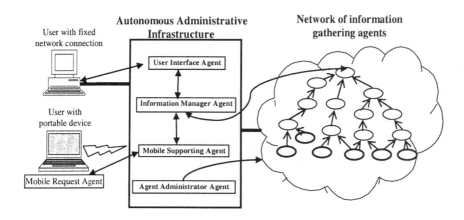

Figure 7-2. General infrastructure of the complete knowledge discovery system

To understand how the autonomous administrative infrastructure works, let's consider a simple scenario (figure 2). A user initiates a query by contacting either a UIA (for users with fixed connection) or a MRA (for users with portable device). The MRA is a mobile agent, located on the portable device, which migrates to the host of MSA and provides it with the user request. The MRA and MSA compensate for the limited capabilities of mobile devices. They provide an interface as the entry point of the mobile network users to the fixed network without a need for high communication traffic. Next, the MSA delegates the request to an IMA (there may be several agents of this type in AAI for multiple concurrent requests), which in turn contacts the appropriate information agent in the network by referring to its directory of domain models (described below). The information agent uses its network, cooperating with other agents in the network (as was described in previous section), constructs the real-time result and sends it back to the IMA. The IMA forces some more formatting of the information and sends it back to the MSA or

UIA to be presented to the user. In case of portable device users, MSA provides MRA with the findings and launches it back to the portable device.

The Agent Administrator (AA) in AAI is used for maintaining information agents and their networks. Through AA the administrator of the system can generate/modify information agents and therefore their links. The administrator can also introduce new application domains to the system using this agent.

A more complex, but similar, administrative infrastructure for a multi-agent system for geospatial information gathering and integration has been successfully designed and developed. The main components of the information and wrapper agents are described in the next section.

4.1 The Knowledge of an Information Agent

Each information agent is specialized to a single application domain and provides access to the available information sources within that domain. Each agent contains an *ontology* of its domain of expertise—its *domain model*—and models of the other agents that can provide relevant information—its *information source models*. The domain model is an ontology that represents the domain of interest of the agent and establishes the terminology for interacting with the agent. The information-source models describe both the contents of the information sources and their relationship to the domain. These models do not need to contain a complete description of the other agents, but rather only those portions that are directly relevant.

The domain model of an agent defines its area of expertise and the terminology for communicating with it. That is, it provides an ontology to describe the application domain. The ontology consists of descriptions of the classes of objects in the domain, relationships between these classes, and other domain-specific information. These classes and relationships do not necessarily correspond directly to the objects described in any particular information source. The model provides a semantic description of the domain, which is used extensively for processing queries.

Each information source model has two main parts. First, there is the description of the contents of the information source. This comprises the concepts of interest available from that information source in terms of the ontology of that information source. The terms in the ontology provide the language that the information source understands. Second, the relationship between these information source concepts and the concepts in the domain model needs to be stated. These mappings are used for transforming a domain model query into a set of queries to the appropriate information sources.

As was mentioned earlier, each information agent in this system is knowledgeable about a single application domain. The domain model is intended to be a description of the application source within that domain. The domain model is intended to be a description of the application domain from point of view of users or other information agents that may need to obtain information about the application domain.

Figure 3 shows a fragment of the domain model of the Sea-Agent that belongs to the organization of figure 1. The nodes represent concepts (i.e., classes of objects), the thick arrows represent subsumption (i.e., subclass relationships), and the thin arrows represent concepts roles (i.e., relationships between classes). Some concepts that specify the range of roles have been left out of the figure for clarity. Some are simple types, such as strings or numbers (such as ship-name), while others are defined concepts (such as geoloc-code).

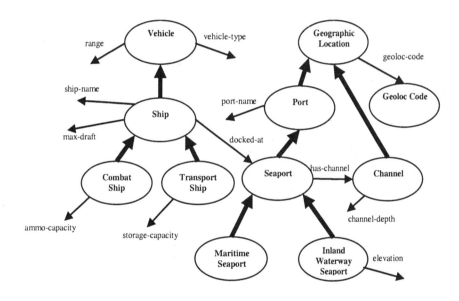

Figure 7-3. Fragment of the Domain Model of the Sea Agent

An agent will have models of several other agents that provide useful information for its domain of expertise. Each information-source model has two main parts. First, there is the description of the contents of the information source. This comprises the concepts of interest available from that information source in terms of the ontology of that information source. The terms in the ontology provide the language that the information source understands (and that will be used to communicate with it). Second, the relationship between these information source concepts and the concepts in the domain model needs to be stated. These mappings are used for transforming a domain model query into a set of queries to the appropriate information sources.

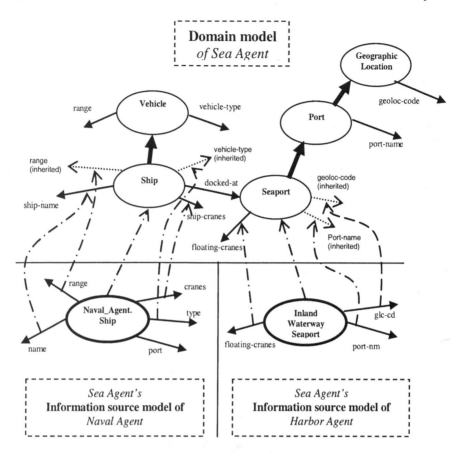

Figure 7-4. Relating an Information-Source Model to a Domain Model (in the Sea Agent)

Figure 4 illustrates how an information source is modeled and how it is related to the domain model. All of the concepts and roles in the information-source model are mapped to concepts and roles in the domain model. A mapping link between two concepts or roles (dashed lines in the figure) indicates that they represent the same class of information; more precisely, their extensions are equivalent. Thus, if the user (of the Sea_Agent) requests all seaports, that information can be retrieved from the concept Harbor of the Harbor_Agent. Note that the domain model may include relationships that involve concepts coming from different agents (like the role docked-at of the ship concept) but are not explicitly present in any one information source.

These knowledge components were first modeled in API-Calculus [34] and then verified and evaluated using ACVisualizer tool, a validation/verification/evaluation tool for API-Calculus [2]. After finalizing the models, they were stated in XML Declarative Description, XDD in short [37]. XDD employs XML as its bare syntax and enhances XML expressions power by employing Declarative Description theory

[3]. A description in XDD is a set of ordinary XML elements, extended XML elements with variables, and the XML elements' relationships in terms of XML clauses. An ordinary XML element denotes a semantic unit and is a surrogate of an information item in the real knowledge domain. An extended XML element corresponds to implicit information or a set of semantic units. Clauses express rules, conditional relationships, integrity constraints, and ontological axioms. XDD is integrated with the Java Expert System Shell [18] to facilitate dynamic representation of domain models and information source models in the system.

In our prototype system, "*geographical and spatial aspects of military logistic planning*" is the knowledge domain of choice for which the network of the intelligent agents is being created. This knowledge domain involves information about the movement of personnel and material from one location to another using aircraft, ship, trucks, etc [31][8][9][23].

4.2   Query processing

A critical capability of an information agent is the ability to flexibly and efficiently retrieve and process data. Query processing requires developing a plan for obtaining the requested data. This includes selecting the information sources to provide the data, the processing operations, the sites where the operations will be performed, and the order in which to perform them. Since data can be moved around between different sites, processed at different locations, and the operations can be performed in a variety of orders, the space of possible plans is quite large.

For the prototype system, we have developed the basis for a flexible planning system to generate and execute query access plans. Some desirable features of the query processor are the ability to execute operations in parallel, to augment and replan queries that fail while executing other queries, and, most interestingly, to gather additional information at runtime to aid the query processing.

The query processing mechanism is being implemented around a query processing unit developed for a geospatial information gathering and integration system [33] which was also used in SWORD, a comprehensive distributed web access juvenile delinquency database (Department of Public Safety-JAIBG Grant).

4.3   Wrapper Agents (Data Repositories)

As described earlier, wrapper agents are information agents that correspond to different data repositories. For each category of data repositories (information source), there will be an intelligent agent with adequate expertise for knowledge discovery.

Wrapper agents are responsible for the system's lowest level knowledge extraction (data mining). These agents are the only information agents that are required to do actual data mining and knowledge discovery over raw data. As was mentioned earlier, other information agents build their knowledge from the knowledge produced by the wrappers or other lower level information agents, which provide them with abstracted information. The steps of the knowledge discovery process, which is carried out by the wrapper agents, are as follows [35]:

- Data Selection: Creating a target data set in its domain expertise
- Data handling
  - Cleaning and preprocessing
  - Data reduction and transformation
- Choosing functions of data mining algorithm(s)
- Data mining: search for patterns of interest
- Pattern evaluation and knowledge presentation in appropriate domain model
  - Transformation, removing redundant patterns, etc.
- Providing discovered knowledge to higher level information agents

Data mining is the core of the knowledge discovery process and includes the following subtasks [35]:

- Cluster analysis: Cluster engine is used for the automated detecting of clusters of records that lie close to each other in a certain sense in the space of all variables. Such clusters may represent different target groups in different domains. The cluster engine places records corresponding to different clusters in separate datasets for further analysis.
- Classification
  - Finding models (functions) that describe and distinguish classes of information
  - Presentation using decision-tree and classification rule
- Association: correlation and causality
- Concept description: characterization and discrimination
  - Generalize, summarize, and contrast data characteristics
- Outlier analysis
  - Outlier is a data object that does not comply with the general behavior of the data
  - It can be considered as noise or an exception but is quite useful in rare event analysis
- Trend and evolution analysis
  - Deviation and regression analysis
  - Sequential pattern mining, periodicity analysis
  - Similarity-based analysis
- Other pattern-directed or statistical analysis

Since the above process may generate many patterns - not all of them are interesting to the system - a final step of *interestingness measurement* is also performed. In the architecture of the wrapper agents, a pattern is interesting if it is understandable by the system based on the domain models, valid with some degree of certainty, potentially useful to the system, novel, or validates some hypothesis that the higher level information agents seek to confirm. The interestingness measurement in wrapper agents is an objective task, based on statistics and structure of the patterns, e.g., support, confidence, etc.

Prototype wrapper agents for vector and raster images have been implemented for our domain of choice (geographical and spatial aspects of military logistic planning). These were developed using previous work in knowledge discovery for the wrapper agents of the geospatial information gathering and integration system, mentioned above [33][38].

4.4 Information Processing in Information Agents

As figure 1 illustrates, the knowledge discovered by the wrapper agents is provided to the higher level information agents in the network for integration and abstraction. Each information agent processes the information it receives from other agents and provides abstract knowledge, consistent with its domain model, which in turn is provided to other agents that request its expertise. This information processing includes the following tasks:

- Data cleaning: smoothes noisy data, removes outliers from its domain model.
- Data integration: Combines data from multiple sources while detecting and resolving data conflicts.
- Data transformation: Data normalization and aggregation by using domain model described earlier.
- Data reduction (abstraction): Obtains reduced representation in volume but produces the same or similar results in its domain model.

These information processing tasks are very similar to the ones implemented for the conflation agents in [33], except that there we were dealing only with geospatial data.

4.5 Learning

An intelligent agent for information gathering should be able to improve both its accuracy and performance over time. To achieve these goals, the information agents will support three forms of learning. First, they should have the capability to cache frequently retrieved or difficult to retrieve information. Second, for those cases where caching is not appropriate, an agent should learn about the contents of the information sources in order to minimize the costs of retrieval. Finally, an information agent should be able to analyze the contents of its information sources in order to refine its domain model to better reflect the currently available information. All these forms of learning can improve the efficiency of the system, and the last one can also improve its accuracy.

4.5.1   Caching Retrieved Data

Data that is required frequently or is very expensive to retrieve can be cached in the local agent and then retrieved more efficiently [4]. An elegant feature of using XDD to model the domain is that cached information can easily be represented and stored in XDD. The data is currently brought into the local agent for processing, so caching is simply a matter of retaining the data and recording what data has been retrieved.

To cache retrieved data into the local agent requires formulating a description of the data so it can be used to answer future queries. This can be extracted from the initial query, which is already expressed in the form of a domain-level description of the desired data. The description defines a new subconcept and it is placed in the appropriate place in the concept hierarchy. The data then become instances of this concept and can be accessed by retrieving all the instances of it.

Once the system has defined a new class and stored the data under this class, the cached information becomes a new information source concept for the agent. The reformulation operations, which map a domain query into a set of information source queries, will automatically consider this new information source. Since the system takes the retrieval costs into account in selecting the information sources, it will naturally gravitate towards using cached information where appropriate. In those cases where the cached data does not capture all of the required information, it may still be cheaper to retrieve everything from the remote site. However, in those cases where the cached information can be used to avoid an external query, the use of the stored information can provide significant efficiency gains.

The use of caching raises a number of important questions, such as which information should be cached and how the cached information is kept up-to-date. We are exploring caching schemes where, rather than caching the answer to a specific query, general classes of frequently used information are stored. This is especially useful in the Internet environment where a single query can be very expensive and the same set of data is often used to answer multiple queries. To avoid problems of information becoming out of date, we have focused on caching relatively static information.

4.5.2   Learning rules for Semantic Query Optimization

The goal of an information agent is to provide efficient access to a set of information sources. Since accessing and processing information can be very costly, the system strives for the best performance that can be provided with the resources available. This means that when it is not processing queries, it gathers information to aid in future retrieval requests [15].

The learning is triggered when an agent detects an expensive query. In this way, the agent will incrementally gather a set of rules to reformulate expensive queries.

The learning subsystem uses induction on the contents of the information sources to construct a less expensive specification of the original query. This new query is then compared with the original to generate a set of rules that describe the relationships between the two equivalent queries. The learned rules are integrated into the agent's domain model and then used for semantic query optimization. These learned rules form an abstract model of the information provided by other agents or data repositories.

4.5.3   Reconciling Agent Models

So far we have assumed that the domain and information-source models of an agent are perfectly aligned. That is, the mappings among concepts in these models perfectly correspond to the actual information. In a network of autonomous agents this assumption will not hold in general. First, the designer of the models might not have had a complete understanding of the semantics of the information provided by each agent. Second, even if at design time the models were accurate, the autonomy of the agents will cause some concepts to drift from their original meaning. The dynamic nature of the information implies that we need to provide mechanisms to detect inconsistency and/or incompleteness in the agent's knowledge. In this section we describe an approach to automatically reconcile agent models, which will improve both the accuracy of the represented knowledge and the efficiency of the information gathering. It consists of three phases. First, an agent checks for misalignments between the domain and source models. Second, it modifies the domain model to represent the new classes of information detected. Third, if possible, it learns from the actual data a description that declaratively describes these new concepts.

We will illustrate the main ideas of this approach through an example from the domain of the Sea Agent (Figure 5). Assume that initially both Harbor_Agent.Harbor and Port_Agent.Port contain the same information about major commercial seaports, which for the purposes of the application is in agreement with the intended semantics of the concept Seaport. However, the Port_Agent evolves to contain information about recreational, small fishing harbors, etc. The Harbor_Agent and Port_Agent are no longer equivalent providers of Seaport information.

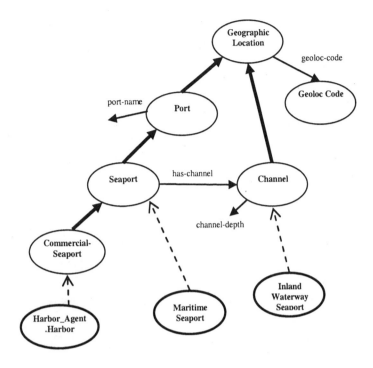

Figure 7-5. Reconciled Model

First, analyzing their actual extensions, our agent will notice that Harbor_Agent.Harbor is now a subset of Port_Agent.Port. Second, the domain model is automatically modified as shown in Figure 5. A new concept Commercial-Seaport is added to the domain model as a subconcept of the original Seaport. Harbor_Agent.Harbour will map now into Commercial-Seaport. Third, we apply machine learning algorithms in order to obtain a concise description of this new concept. For example, it might construct a description that distinguishes commercial seaports from generic seaports by the number of cranes available. With this refined model, a query like "retrieve all the seaports that have more than 15 cranes and channels more than 70 feet deep", which describes information only satisfied by commercial seaports, could be appropriately directed to the Harbor_Agent, saving both in communication (less data transmitted) and processing costs (less data considered in any subsequent join), because the concept Harbor has a smaller number of instances. Moreover, a query about a small craft harbor will not be incorrectly directed to the Harbor_Agent, but to the Port_Agent which is the only one that can provide such information.

4.5.4   Control and Coordination

Ultimately, control and coordination will be key issues in multi-agent systems for real-time information discovery and integration. Real-time constraints generally require that problem solving be approximate and satisfying, where certain aspects of the quality of the results (e.g., breadth or precision) must be traded-off to meet the imposed time constraints. In addition to being a multi-attribute decision problem, control here also involves considerable uncertainty. The quality characteristics of results for any query can be predicted only approximately, and the response times and even availability of information sources can be highly variable and dynamic. This can require that sources and methods be adjusted in real-time, or that additional information sources be exploited if results prove unsatisfactory. Making such control decisions can be extremely complex, since the behaviors of multiple agents will need to be coordinated.

For example, should one agent/source prove to be unacceptably slow in providing results for a detailed subquery, it may be desirable to modify that agent's subquery. This will also require that other agents' subqueries be modified as is appropriate to best meet the overall system goals. As discussed in query processing section, query planning largely ignores these issues initially, by assuming that providing agents can make good predictions, in their domains, about performance, etc. However, the question of what approaches to control and coordination are most appropriate for multi-agent real-time information discovery and integration need to be considered. In our prototype network, we have not considered this issue, but for the next version, we will consider both heuristic approaches such as real-time planners [6,7,25], as well as formal methods such as decentralized Markov decision problems [26,36].

5.   CONCLUSION

Information sources are becoming more diverse and more technically capable. Because of fast advancing information technology, scientists, educators, and decision makers are facing much more complex and detailed questions. To answer these questions, they need to be multidisciplinary experts or have access to experts in many specialized disciplines. The proposed system models the above relationship by using intelligent agents and distributing the knowledge discovery process on a particular domain among multiple agents responsible for different sub-domains.

A prototype system based on the proposed architecture has been implemented. In our prototype, "geographical and spatial aspects of military logistic planning" is the knowledge domain of choice for which a preliminary network of three wrapper and five information agents has been created at SIUC Software Agent Lab.

6. REFERENCES

1. Ackerman, M. S., Starr, B., and Pazzani, M., 1997, The Do-I-Care agent: Effective social discovery and filtering on the Web, *Proceedings of RIAO Computer-Assisted InformationSearching on the Internet*, pp. 17-31.
2. Ahmad, R., Ali, D., Cobb, M., and Rahimi, S., 2003, A visualization tool for the intelligent agent modeling language API-calculus, *Proceedings of the 9th Annual International Conference on Industry, Engineering, and Management Systems*, pp. 482-488.
3. Akama, K., 1993, Declarative semantics of logic programs on parameterized representation systems, *Advances in Software Science and Technology*, Iwanami Shoten Publications and Academic Press, Tokyo, vol. 5, pp. 45-63.
4. Arens, Y., Knobock, C. A., 1994, Intelligent caching: Selecting, representing, and reusing data in an information server, *Proceedings of the third International and Conference on Information and Knowledge Management*, Gaithersburg, MD, pp.123-131.
5. Bollacker, K., Lawrence, S. and Giles, L., 1998, CiteSeer: An autonomous Web agent for automatic retrieval and identification of interesting publications, *Proceedings of the 2nd International ACM Conference on Autonomous Agents*, pp. 116-123.
6. Carver, N. and Lesser, V., 1993, A planner for the control of problem-solving systems, *IEEE Transactions on Systems, Man, and Cybernetics, Special Issue on Planning, Scheduling and Control*, vol. 23, # 6, pp. 1519-1536.
7. Carver, N. and Lesser, V., 2003, Domain monotonicity and the performance of local solutions strategies for CDPS-based distributed sensor interpretation, *Journal of Autonomous Agents and Multi-Agent Systems*, vol. 6, # 1, pp. 35-76.
8. Chung, M., Wilson, R., Cobb, M., Petry, F. and Shaw, K., 2001, Querying multiple data sources via an object-oriented spatial query interface and framework, *Journal of Visual Languages and Computing,* vol. 12, #1, pp 37-60.
9. Cobb, M., Petry, F., Wen, L. and Yang, H., 2003, Design of system for managing fuzzy relationships for integration of spatial data, *Fuzzy Sets and Systems*, vol. 140, # 1, pp. 51-73.
10. Davis, J., Week, R. and Revett, C., 1999, Information agents for world wide Web. *BT Technology Journal*, vol. 14, #4, pp. 105-114.
11. Doorenbos, R. B., Etzioni, O. and Weld, D. S., 1997, A scalable comparison-shopping agent or the World-Wide Web, *Proceedings of the First International Conference on Autonomous Agent*, pp. 39–48.
12. Eirinaki, M. and Vazirgianis, M., 2003, Web mining for Web personalization, *ACM Transactions on Internet Tehnology (TOIT)*, vol. 3, #1, pp. 1-27.
13. Etzioni, O. and Weld, D., 1994, A SoftBot-based interface to the Internet, *Communication of the ACM*, vol 37, #7, pp. 72–76.
14. Fisher, D., Soderland, S., McCarthy, J., Feng, F., and Lehnert, W., 1996, Description of the UMass systems as used for MUC-6, *Proceedings of the 6th Message Understanding onference*.
15. Hsu, C. N., Knoblock, C. A., 1995, Using inductive learning to generate rules for semantic query optimization, in: Advances in: *Knowledge Discovery and Data Mining*, G. P. Shapiro and U. Fayyad, ed., MIT Press, Chapter 17.
16. Hu, C. L. and Chen W. E., 1998, Mobile agents collaboration for information gathering. *Workshop on Distributed System Technologies & Applications*, NCKU, R.O.C, pp. 537-546.
17. Jamsa, K., Lalani, S. and Weakley, S., 1996, *Web Programming*, Jamsa Press.
18. Jess Manual 6.1, 2003, The Java Expert System Shell, *URL: http://herzberg..ca.sandia. gov/jess*.

19. Joachims, T., Freitag, D. and Mitchell, T., 1997, Webwatcher: A tour guide for the world wide Web. *Proceedings of the Fifteenth International Joint Conference on Artificial Intelligence*, pp. 770–775.

20. Kenoblock, C. A., 1995, Planning, executing, sensing, and replanning for information gathering, *Proceedings of the Fourteenth International Joint Conference on Artificial Intelligence*, pp. 1686–1693.

21. Kenoblock, C.A. and Ambite, J.L., 1997, Agents for Information Gathering, *Software Agents*, J. Bradshaw, ed., MIT Press, Menlo Park, Calif.

22. Kwok, C. T. and Weld, D. S., 1996, Planning to gather information, *Proceedings of the Thirteenth National Conference on Artificial Intelligence*, pp. 32–39.

23. Ladner, R., Petry, F., Cobb, M., 2003, Fuzzy set approaches to spatial data mining of association rules, *Transactions on GIS*, vol. 7, #1, pp. 123-138.

24. Leberman. H., 1995, Letizia: A agent that assists Web browsing, *Proceedings of the Fourteenth International Joint Conference on Artificial Intelligence*, pp. 924–929.

25. Lesser, V., Horling, B., Klassner, F., Raja, A., Wagner, T., and Zhang, S., 2000, BIG: An agent for resource-bounded information gathering and decision making, *Artificial ntelligence Journal*, Special Issue on Internet Information Agents, vol. 118, # 1-2, pp. 197- 44.

26. Lesser, V., Decker, K., Wagner, T., Carver, N., Garvey, A., Horling, B., Neiman, D., Podorozhny, R., Prasad, M., Raja, A., Vincent, R., Xuan, P., and Zhang, XQ., 2004, Evolution of the GPGP/TAEMS domain-independent coordination framework, To appear in *Journal of Autonomous Agents and Multi-Agent Systems*.

27. Martin, D., Morgan, D., Gohama, H. and Cheyer, A., 1997, Information brokering in an agent architecture, *Proceeding of the Second International Conference on the Practical Application of Intelligent Agents and Multi-Agent Technology*, pp. 467-486.

29. Matsatsinis, N.F., Moratis, P., Psomatakis, V., Spanoudakis, N., 1999, An intelligent software agent framework for decision support systems development, *Proceedings of European Symposium on Intelligent Techniques*. Greece, pp 134-139.

30. Menczer, F., 1997, ARACHNID: Adaptive retrieval agents choosing heuristic neighborhoods for information discovery, *Proceedings of the Fourteenth International Conference on Machine Learning*, pp. 227–235.

31. Murray, B. H., 2000, Sizing the Internet, A Cyveillance White Paper, *URL: http://www.cyveillance.com/web/downloads /Sizing_the_Internet.pdf.*

32. Petry, F., Cobb, M., Rahimi, S., Ali, D., Paprzycki, M., and Angryk, R., 2002, Fuzzy spatial relationships and mobile agent technology in geospatial information systems, *Soft Computing in Defining Spatial Relations*, volume in series: Soft Computing, Edited by Pascal Matsakis, and Les M. Sztandera, Phsica-Verlag, pp. 123-155.

33. Rahimi, S., Ali, A. and Ali, D., 2001, An investigation on intelligent software-agent technology, *Proceeding for IEMS and IC&IE 2001 joint international conference*, Florida, pp. 84-90.

34. Rahimi, S., Cobb, M., Ali, D., Paprzycki, M.and Petry, F., 2002a, A knowledge-based multi-agent system for geospatial data conflation, *Journal of Geographic Information and Decision Analysis*, vol. 6, # 2, p.p 67-81.

35. Rahimi, S., Cobb, M., Ali, D. and Petry, F., 2002b, A modeling tool for intelligent-agent based systems: Api-calculus, *Soft Computing Agents: A New Perspective for Dynamic Systems,* the International Series "Frontiers in Artificial Intelligence and Application," Edited by Vincenzo Loia, IOS Press, pp. 165-186.

36. Rahimi, S., 2003, Data mining: concepts and technology, Technical Report, Southern Illinois University, Carbondale.

37. Shen, J., Lesser, V., Carver, N., 2003, Minimizing communication cost in a distributed bayesian network using a decentralized MDP, *Proceedings of Second International Joint Conference on Autonomous Agents and MultiAgent Systems*, pp. 678-685.

38. Wuwongse, W., Anutariya, C., Akama, K., and Nantajeewarawat, E., 2001, XML declarative description (XDD): A language for semantic web, *IEEE Intelligent Systems*, vol. 16, # 3, pp. 54-65.

39. Zhou, H, Rahimi, S., Wang, Y. and Cobb, M., 2004, A task-oriented compositional mobile agent architecture for knowledge exchange between agencies and agent, *Informatica Journal, Special Issue on Agent-Based Computing,* pp. 23-30, Vol. 28, No.1.

Chapter 8

NATURAL ENVIRONMENT DATA SERVICES IN DISTRIBUTED MODELING AND SIMULATION

Joseph B. Collins and Christopher G. Scannell
The Naval Research Laboratory, Information Technology Division, Advanced Information Technlogy Branch, 4555 Overlook Avenue, SW, Washington, DC 20375

Abstract: In this chapter we describe current and future solutions to providing representations of the natural environment to modeling and simulation (M&S) architectures. Two recently developed applications we describe are the Ocean, Atmospheric, and Space Environmental Services (OASES) federate and the Acoustic Transmission Loss Server (ATLoS) federate. These applications, working in concert with the Navy's Tactical Environmental Data Services, TEDServices, exemplify the current practice of distributing environmental data services to Navy M&S. Our experience with developing and using these applications within the current M&S interoperability framework, the High Level Architecture and Run-Time Interface (HLA/RTI), have led us to begin to develop a newer representation scheme for environmental models: an ontology of physics. An ontology of physics provides a more abstract semantic description scheme for representing both models of the natural environment and their data. Nothing less than a full ontology of physics will do to represent semantic information because Department of Defense (DoD) systems that are operationally sensitive to environmental conditions are in space, the atmosphere, and the ocean and require representation of fluid dynamics, thermodynamics, electrodynamics, quantum mechanics, and even general relativity.

Key Words: High Level Architecture, Run-time Infrastructure, federation, Fleet Battle Experiment, synthetic natural environment, ontology, physics, modeling and simulation, markup language, OASES, TEDServices, ATLoS,

1.   INTRODUCTION AND BACKGROUND

Distributed Modeling and Simulation (M&S) is a burgeoning area of research and development in support of analysis, planning, training, experimentation, and doctrine development activities for U.S. Department of Defense (DoD), Homeland Security, Emergency Management, and Coalition partnerships. Distributed M&S enables world-wide, interactive participation and shared experiences via these activities.

A key element for supporting realism in representing the functions of simulated objects and systems is the representation of the state of the natural environment of the world, in particular the global dynamic states due to the atmosphere, ocean, and space. These elements of the true natural environment have profound effects on the operation of sensor and communication systems as well as impacting the accessibility of remote locations, so, consequently, accurate representation of these elements and their interactions with models of these systems is essential. In representing these aspects of the environment we need to keep in mind the question, "How much is enough?", in relation to the accuracy and the meaning of the representations we are communicating.

1.1   Current State of M&S Communication Protocols

The 1990's saw a rapid development of Distributed Interactive Simulation (DIS) applications and a corresponding DIS Protocol Data Unit (PDU) was developed and used to communicate interaction data between networked simulation models. Commonly, though not exclusively, the nature of these DIS PDUs was to represent discrete physical interactions between simulated physical entities, such as the exchange of missiles or communications. The DIS protocol evolved into the High Level Architecture (HLA) and its implementation, the Run-Time Infrastructure (RTI) with the structure of the information packets exchanged now being captured in a simulation Federation Object Model (FOM). The FOM is defined so that all of the federates in an M&S federation may share a common description of the network communications traffic. The HLA/RTI, which uses an underlying Common Object Request Broker Architecture, or CORBA framework, defines all of the simulation object services and simulation time management services that a simulation federation will use. We will describe in the next few sections how the OASES and ATLoS federates work within this architecture to deliver environmental representations provided by Navy and other DoD environmental models.

1.2   Future state of M&S Communication Protocols

Concurrent with the rapid development of the DIS and HLA/RTI architectures and applications was the emergence of the world-wide web. As the web developed the flood of information available raised the question, "What does it all mean?" This is far from being a philosophical question. The enormity of the information on the web forces us to consider how to better structure documents so that searching, accessing, and interpreting them is more manageable. The development of the Semantic Web promises to help us do these things. Additionally, while the web has initially been dominated by documents, in the future services will be as important if not more important than documents. Anticipating this, we describe in later sections how M&S services for representing the natural environment, and, indeed, services for representing the behaviors of physics-based models in general, might look in the future.

2.   OASES

The Total Atmosphere Ocean Services (TAOS) system [1] was developed as part of the Defense Advanced Research Projects Agency (DARPA) Synthetic Theater of War (STOW) to provide a single consistent representation of the natural environment to simulation entities interacting in a DIS or HLA-based simulation. This environmental server evolved into the Ocean, Atmospheric, and Space Environmental Services (OASES) system as part of the Defense Modeling and Simulation Office's (DMSO) Environment Federation (EnviroFed) project [2]. The EnviroFed project focused on developing a reference FOM for the environment of sufficient scope to meet the DoD Modeling and Simulation requirements and to demonstrate an environmental server capable of serving to a heterogeneous HLA federation a single environment composed of objects attributed and classified according to the DMSO-developed international standard, Environmental Data Coding Specification, part of the Synthetic Environment Data Representation and Interchange Specification (SEDRIS).

The Navy Warfare Development Command (NWDC) was the first organization that adopted the use of OASES consistently as part of their standard operating procedure for M&S with their Fleet Battle Experiments [3] which were conducted with the U.S. Navy Fleets to develop new doctrine, concepts and tactics as well as to help evaluate future Navy force structure. An accurate representation of the ocean's temperature and salinity as a function of depth was required to model the propagation of underwater sound so as to simulate accurate detection ranges for simulated submarines. This was particularly important as these experiments simultaneously involved use of live and virtual forces in close proximity, so significant differences between data and direct observation could be telling.

After decades of unrelenting anti-submarine warfare (ASW) activities in the North Atlantic during the Cold War, the focus of the Navy shifted away from ASW with the dissolution of the Soviet Union. Now ASW has again become one of the U.S. Navy's top priorities, but the operating environment has shifted to a much more complex environment, the littorals. In improving Navy capability via experimentation, technology development, and training, the focus is on: moving away from platform-intensive concepts of operation; reducing the time required to detect enemy submarines; and planning for a future in which there will be advanced weapons using precise localization and distributed, networked forces, heavily equipped with remote sensors, all organized according to the latest "capability-based planning" approaches devised by the DoD.

Fleet Battle Experiment – Kilo (FBE-K), in conjunction with exercise Tandem Thrust 2003, was carried out by NWDC in cooperation with the U.S. Navy's Seventh Fleet, and was the eleventh in a series of FBEs. Figure 8-1 illustrates the manner in which the synthetic natural environment (SNE) was provided to and used by the FBE-K simulation. The environmental data providers ran the Navy environmental models whose model outputs constituted the SNE for FBE-K. This data was delivered to the modeling and simulation network via a TEDServices gateway. The OASES Publisher federate [2] published the model data to the HLA federation. The Acoustic Transmission Loss Server (ATLoS), an HLA federate and client of OASES, used the spatially and temporally varying environmental parameters to field acoustic transmission loss calculation requests made by entities within the Joint Semi-Automated Forces (JSAF) federates [4], [5]. The Integrated Modeling Platform with Agent-Controlled Tasking federate, the other client of OASES for FBE-K, used atmospheric environmental parameters to model aerosol dispersion using the Gaussian Puff model.

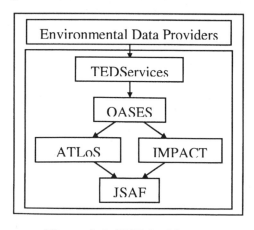

Figure 8-1. SNE Architecture

2.1   Navy Environmental Models

The data required to construct the SNE was acquired from three primary sources: the Naval Oceanographic Office (NAVOCEANO), the Fleet Numerical Meteorology and Oceanography Center (FNMOC) and the Naval Research Laboratory (NRL) divisions at the Stennis Space Center (NRL-Stennis), specifically the Oceanography Division.

The majority of the ocean-related parameters used in FBE-K came from NAVOCEANO. NAVOCEANO is the principal source of tailored oceanographic support to the joint DoD forces operation in the littoral zone. NAVOCEANO maintains a suite of standard Navy databases of historic data into which a comprehensive set of non-real-time oceanographic, hydrographic data from in-situ surveys are injected. NAVOCEANO also processes data from several satellites and manages the Navy's oceanographic data fusion initiatives.

FNMOC, in Monterey, CA, is the principal operational processing center for automated numerical meteorological and oceanographic (METOC) analyses and predictions for the DoD. Their global and regional models treat the coupled air-ocean environment as a totally integrated system and pay particular attention to the air-ocean interface. FNMOC receives global environmental data through links with DoD and the National Oceanic and Atmospheric Administration data-distribution systems. Their operation products are distributed on Navy and joint command-and-control systems via the Navy theater METOC centers, which then develop value-added products and services tailored to specific military operations in their areas of responsibility. Their products tend to be run over large areas, such as global models or large regional models, e.g. the Mediterranean.

The Oceanographic Division at NRL-Stennis, located in Stennis, MS, is the major center for in-house Navy research and development in oceanography. They operate worldwide experimental programs to validate their numerical models. When their models are sufficiently mature, they are transitioned to NAVOCEANO, to FNMOC, or to one of the six Navy regional centers all under the guidance of the Commander, Naval Meteorology and Oceanography.

The atmospheric regime was modeled as well as the ocean regime during FBE-K. The Coupled Ocean Atmosphere Prediction System (COAMPS) is an analysis-nowcast and forecast tool applicable for any given region of the earth [6]. It was developed at NRL-Monterey and is run operationally at FNMOC. COAMPS forecasts parameters up to 48 hours out, at one to three hour increments. Modeled parameters include precipitation, atmospheric pressure, air temperature, relative humidity, vapor pressure, latent heat flux, sensible heat flux, solar radiation, infrared flux, wind velocity, and wind stress. COAMPS is currently running operationally in a nested configuration, with the outer grid using a 27-km grid spacing and the inner grid a 9-km spacing.

The Modular Ocean Data Assimilation System (MODAS) is one of the current Navy standard tools for the production of three-dimensional forecast grids of ocean temperature and salinity, and derived quantities such as density, sound speed, mixed layer depth, sonic layer depth, depth excess, deep sound channel axis, and critical depth. Developed by NRL-Stennis and run by operationally by NAVOCEANO, MODAS was designed to combine observed ocean data with climatological information to produce a quality-controlled, gridded forecast as its output [7].

The Navy Coastal Ocean Model (NCOM) was developed at NRL-Stennis. The 1/8° global NCOM is run daily at NAVOCEANO to produce nowcasts and forecasts of the ocean temperature and salinity throughout the water column. The atmospheric forcing data used for NCOM is the Navy Operational Global Atmospheric Prediction System. The model also assimilates sea surface temperature and synthetic temperature and salinity profiles from the MODAS model. Lastly, NCOM integrates the sea surface heights from the output of the operational 1/16° global NRL Layered Ocean Model as well as the sea surface temperatures from the output of the 1/8° MODAS two-dimensional nowcasts.

In addition to using the outputs of models that predict the atmospheric conditions, COAMPS, and models that predict the temperature and salinity of the ocean volume, MODAS and NCOM, information about the ocean surface was required. The primary use of this data for FBE-K was to estimate the impact of the surface roughness of the ocean on the transmission of acoustic energy. The Navy's Wave Action Model (WAM) is a spectral wave prediction model developed by the WAMDI Group [8] and run operationally by NAVOCEANO. Typically, WAM produces a directional spectrum of energy density in 25 frequency bins and in 24 15-degree wide directional sectors from which significant wave height, average wave period, and average wave direction can be computed [9]. In FBE-K the significant wave height, defined as the average height of the highest one-third of the waves in a particular region, was used by the ATLoS federate to estimate the surface roughness.

2.2   Model Data Delivery

Procuring the model data needed for a simulation can be a time-consuming task, particularly if the need is for a reliable delivery of data from an external agency over an extended period of time. The Navy fleets have a requirement for timely METOC data such as the model data just discussed.

Logically, then, it would be very practical for a DoD simulation to make use of the same model data delivery mechanism used by the operational fleet.

2.3 Model Data Delivery to the Fleet

The centerpiece of the shipboard suite of METOC equipment is the Tactical Environmental Support System (TESS), which provides tailored meteorological, electro-magnetic propagation, oceanographic, acoustic, and satellite products in direct support of Fleet air and surface planning and operations and ASW operations. Specifically, TESS provides the capability to assess the effects of the environment on fleet sensors, platforms, and weapons systems. Data sources include in-situ sensors, geostationary and polar-orbiting satellites, U.S. and foreign weather broadcasts, and three-dimensional weather and oceanic data fields prepared ashore.

The Navy Integrated Tactical Environmental Sub-system (NITES) is a modular, open-architecture software sub-system of TESS that is integrated as a segment of the Navy C4I system on board all ships and at all major Navy/Marine Corps commands and staffs, both ashore and afloat. NITES integrates TESS-derived products into command and control tactical decision aids for use with strategic and tactical computer systems on smaller ships and sites.

During FBE-K the ships of the 7th fleet used NITES to receive delivery of METOC model data, such as COAMPS output. Some of the ships received the data through the Navy's TEDServices system. TEDServices, a very recent follow-on to the Navy's Tactical Environmental Data Server (TEDS), a METOC information storage and management system created under the sponsorship of the Oceanographer of the Navy (N096). TEDServices was created to replace TEDS and is currently under development. Each of the ships using TEDServices during FBE-K had installed on-board a TEDServices gateway and a tactical decision aid, such as the latest version of NITES, NITES II Object-Oriented Redesign (OOR). NITES II OOR and other tactical systems using TEDServices were tightly integrated with the TEDServices gateways and directly accessed their databases through a public application program interface (API).

2.4 Model Data Delivery to the M&S Network

TEDServices was chosen as the means for receiving nowcasts of the ocean and atmospheric environment for FBE-K and continues to be the approach by which NWDC carries out exercises in-situ exercises where live, virtual and constructed entities are in close proximity. For FBE-K, TEDServices was prescribed by N096 as the delivery mechanism for NCOM model data. TEDServices was also a useful source of COAMPS model data. WAM model data was not available. We received the WAM data, run by NAVOCEANO, but provided to us through NRL-Stennis. Since FBE-K, NWDC has installed its own TEDServices server to facilitate its use of TEDServices in future in-situ experimental exercises.

3.   ATLoS: A SONAR ENVIRONMENTAL EFFECTS SERVER

Over the last several years the representation of the natural environment in simulations, such as with the Semi-Automated Forces, have steadily improved. The improved representation of the ocean environment in particular has been due to a focused Synthetic Natural Environments effort [10].

The Navy is interested in an accurate and relatively high precision characterization of the natural environment, and in particular the ocean environment, because of its impact on sensor systems, particularly sonars. Having a high fidelity characterization of the environment allows the Navy to predict the environment's impact on sensor system performance, allowing the Navy to plan accordingly. The Navy uses these predictions in several ways: in trainers where sensor system operators may experience realistic system performance without having to go to sea; in experimentation where tactical, operational, and strategic doctrine may be developed for new ships and systems before they are deployed; and in analysis, where systems are evaluated for cost and effectiveness before they are acquired and deployed.

As part of this improvement in natural environment representations the Naval Research Lab has developed a federated sonar environmental acoustic effects server, called ATLoS [4, 5], to support multiple sonar types. ATLoS supports models of long range and multi-frequency sonars. ATLoS computes the environmentally dependent acoustic propagation for each source/receiver pair using a range-dependent broadband underwater acoustic propagation model, called FeyRay. FeyRay was developed specifically for real-time applications such as servers. ATLoS is responsible for regularly updating the propagation loss for the longer range, lower frequency sonars. Dynamic, environmental data required by FeyRay are retrieved by ATLoS from the OASES oceanographic data server. These data include oceanographic temperature and salinity profiles and surface condition descriptions. Bottom depth data and bottom type descriptions are obtained by interrogating static terrain representation databases.

OASES, a server we have already described, provides an environmental state. ATLOS, on the other hand, is an environmental effects server. An environmental effects server focuses on representing the significant effects of the natural environment on simulated phenomena, for example, on artificially generated energy emissions, which are emitted, detected, and used by sensor systems like sonars and radars.

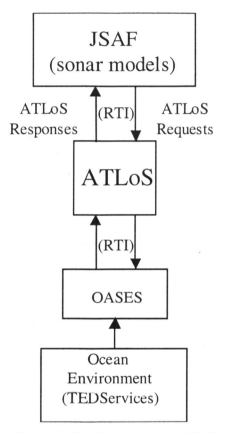

Figure 8-2. Dataflow to and from ATLoS.

3.1 **ATLoS Concept**

The ATLoS environmental acoustic effects server is designed to operate as an HLA federate in a distributed simulation system. It responds to requests from sensor models to predict the effects of the environment on a sensor, i.e., the transmission loss, and it maintains a current state estimate of the environmental variables that affect the class of sensors that use the effects server. At a later date we may augment the server with additional effects, such as a detailed reverberation calculation. The architecture by which ATLoS serves its function is illustrated in Figure 2.

The objective of the ATLoS development effort was to implement and test a flexible environmental effects server which could provide data fast enough to operate in real-time in an HLA simulation environment, yet be accurate enough to faithfully simulate the acoustic transmissions received by sonar systems among the federates. ATLoS, as a server, contains within it multiple components. It contains the fast, reasonably accurate, marine acoustic propagation model called FeyRay. ATLoS also contains rapidly accessible, three-dimensional databases of the necessary environmental acoustic data. Thirdly, ATLoS contains a component called KingKong, which serves as an interface between the other components and the incoming requests from the sonar models. Finally, there is an RTI interaction manager that queues incoming requests and dispatches responses. ATLoS interacts during simulation time with the external OASES server over the RTI. FeyRay requires, as input, oceanographic environmental acoustic data that OASES provides, such as sound speed derived from temperature, salinity, and pressure. These environmental data are site-specific and, being dynamic, are time-specific and so they are updated as a function of time during the simulation. Finally, ATLoS receives requests from sonar models for the environmental response it provides, and responds to those requests, over the same RTI.

ATLoS currently interacts with other federates in a simulation environment with JSAF federates. Since many of the libraries that comprise JSAF also support the necessary functionality of an HLA federate on the RTI, we used those libraries in creating ATLoS. Those JSAF libraries include the Agile FOM Interface, libenv, as well as support for many of the basic data types and classes in JSAF. In addition to these pre-existing JSAF libraries, some new ones were created to implement the above described functions, including libkingkong, libfeyray, libkkio, libSIHAtlosRequest, and libsihatlosresponse. These libraries are maintained at the United States Joint Forces Command.

3.2   Synthetic Natural Environment and ATLoS Results

The fully integrated system has undergone a series of tests in collaboration with NWDC during Fleet Battle Experiments and subsequent experiments. For example, ATLoS has been tested in the laboratory and in the Fleet Battle Experiment-J (FBE-J), part of Millennium Challenge 02 (MC02) as well as in FBE-K and subsequent simulations. ATLoS responds to requests from the JSAF native sonar models, returning transmission loss values with rare failures.

Our team had previously developed a capability to bring a synthetic natural environment to HLA-based simulations [10]. We have used that same capability in testing ATLoS. For example, FBE-J took place in an ocean environment off the coast of Camp Pendleton, CA, between Los Angeles and San Diego. We used the Estuarine and Coastal Ocean Model (ECOM), a shallow water variant of the Princeton Ocean Model, to model the shallow water environment and the MODAS model data for the deeper water. ECOM runs on a curvilinear grid tailored for the experiment, and is driven at its boundaries by MODAS, North Pacific Ocean Nowcast / Forecast System, and COAMPS. The output data from ECOM is ingested by the OASES federate, which sent out environmental data over the RTI through the course of the simulation.

We have seen extremely high volumes of requests prior to MC02, over 50 per second. ATLoS may drop requests under very high request volume. As new requests arrive corresponding to a given acoustic source / receiver pair, ATLoS drops the old request and maintains a single current transmission loss request for each pair, and these requests proceed through the ATLoS processing queue, guaranteeing fairness for each source/receiver pair. The JSAF native sonar models are tolerant of response lapses from ATLoS, using the last available transmission loss response for a given source/receiver pair when these lapses occur.

We have continued to improve the performance of ATLOS, for example. reducing I/O, streamlining some of the complex transmission loss computations, modifying client behavior to prune unnecessary requests, and making ATLOS a distributed server. We anticipate that the already high rate of requests will increase further, so these efforts are necessary.

4.   TOWARDS AN ONTOLOGY OF PHYSICS

The next step beyond the current state of the art in representing the natural environment is to provide more depth to the data that are exchanged and to the models used to generate that data. The ideas discussed here represent a synthesis of prior work [11, 12]. Many of the assumptions internal to interacting models are not expressed, to the point where one may begin to seriously question the degree of interoperability provided by the communication protocols. We cannot easily use the data as intended without communicating these assumptions using a common language. Meaningful interoperability between physics-based models of the natural environment requires a common understanding and standardized description of the physical laws governing physical objects, i.e., an ontology of physics and the resulting metadata.

We define an ontology as a controlled vocabulary defining a set of concepts, along with their relationships, that are necessary to capture the semantic level information about a domain. For example, currently, the Synthetic Environment Data Representation and Interchange Specification (SEDRIS) [13] standard addresses the description of model data objects, their spatiotemporal coordinates, and many physical attributes. It forms an example of an ontology. We do not see it as complete. What is not described in SEDRIS are model dynamics, i.e., how a model evolves in time between the discrete states that are represented in SEDRIS data transmittals. If model dynamics are not specified with the data, a data recipient will be required to infer how he/she should use the received data, making an inference that will vary depending on the recipient.

Of the many factors that may affect model dynamics, such as military doctrine, human behavior, or physics, we focus on representing physical dynamics. This is commonly a necessary aspect of model dynamics, particularly in representing the natural environment. The key concepts in representing physical dynamics are the equations of physics, usually phrased as differential equations, and how they relate to static representations of physical objects, such as those represented in SEDRIS. We are beginning to frame the structure of how to incorporate considerations of dynamics in an ontology of physics and beginning to detail the types of physical dynamical relationships that may be modeled.

4.1   Interoperability

Interoperability between modules in an M&S framework is only meaningful to the degree that modules have an accessible description of what they are and what can be done with them. By accessible we mean that other modules, perhaps even humans, can access and interpret the description. The degree of interoperability will be determined by how well the description provides a common, unambiguous understanding. For the highest levels of interoperability we require common conceptual models to support semantic consistency across models [14].

Since some objectives of M&S are to simulate a large range of things that can happen in the real-world, the conceptual framework and language for phrasing such a description, i.e., the ontology, can conceivably cover all of human experience. Since much of what could be described, particularly that which involves mental states, is perhaps subjective, or perhaps not definitively modeled, there will be difficulties in developing standardized comprehensive ontologies for M&S. On the other hand, there are concepts that are objective. In particular, the physical environment can be objectively modeled as can projections of the physical world onto physical sensors. Since many models focus primarily on representing the physical aspects of objects, it would be advantageous to develop an ontology of the physical world. To support interoperability, a standardized ontology is required.

A common M&S system paradigm is of interlinked dynamical models passing each other datagrams representing object state information. The SEDRIS standard was developed for the representation of physical, environmental objects as such datagrams. By its design, SEDRIS enables representation of the state of many, if not most, physical objects. In common M&S architectures, SEDRIS transmittals typically represent static snapshots of the physical state of an object (or the world), which are created and used by algorithmic representations of object dynamics. SEDRIS supports description of model data, but the algorithmic software modules of object dynamics that pass data to each other cannot be similarly described as there is currently no standardized way to do so.

Even though domain experts may share a common background understanding of a given model, when they develop dynamical models in software, various assumptions they make are usually kept hidden, even from other domain experts. If internal representations are hidden from other domain experts, there is little hope that simulation modules will be able to communicate a description to each other, module to module. The ability of software modules to communicate what they do is essential for interoperability. The problem now is, even if domain experts wanted to encode a description of the underlying dynamics and assumptions that they make in their algorithmic representations of physical object dynamics, there is no standard language or semantic reference frame for them to use to do so.

4.2 Ontologies

Domain experts already share an understanding of the common laws of physics; they are taught a common set of concepts in academic physics courses. This understanding, however, is based on informal conventions; we know of no comprehensive, formal standard. For example, International Standards Organization (ISO) physics standards [15] focus on specifying physical units, measurement methods, and the values of fundamental constants. Because there are an arbitrary number of units for specifying the amount of mass an object has, an ISO standard specifies which unit shall be used. Even though multiple reference units are possible, there is but a single concept of mass, a single concept of charge, etc. We see as a shortcoming of these standards that they do not focus on describing mathematical relationships between physical concepts.

SEDRIS references and incorporates many of the ISO physics concepts. Many of the fundamental relationships between concepts, however, such as between mass, force, and acceleration, remain unstated. The underlying relationships between concepts are generally taken for granted as being commonly known. Many of these concepts are the mathematical relations specifying how the physical dynamics of objects are determined by their physical attributes and the physical relationships they have with other objects. What is required is a structure for describing these relationships: such a structure is often called an ontology.

As we have stated, an ontology is a controlled vocabulary defining a set of concepts, along with their relationships, that are necessary to capture the semantic level information about a domain. It is a formal explicit description of concepts, their properties, relationships between the concepts, and the allowed values that they may take. An ontology together with a set of individual instances of classes constitutes a knowledge base [16]. An ontology provides a semantic reference frame useful for automating the communication of abstract information. The purpose of an ontology is to enable the communication of meaning for purposes of understanding. Not all ontologies are equal, however. They depend on the definitions used for "meaning" and "understanding" where understanding is achieved through common usages. It will support the addition of descriptive tags to existing terms, describing assumptions, contextual and other information that often goes unexpressed due to the lack of a formal structure for making such expression. The meaning of those terms in an ontology is largely operational; it depends on the use we expect to make of an ontology.

One conclusion we can quickly make is that an ontology of physics would need to be a widely agreed-upon standard in order to achieve wide interoperability. While expanding a search for consensus may conceivably add new requirements for an ontology, the effort is nevertheless worthwhile in order to achieve broad interoperability. It is difficult to anticipate the interests and consequent requirements of a broader community without directly engaging with them in the development of standards that they would have an interest in using. We believe that for an ontology of physics we should work towards a standard for the Web as a whole, engaging the talents of many contributors, rather than to only support, for example, a DoD M&S intranet. Before engaging in the process of consensus building we will attempt to flesh out a strawman set of requirements and an approach to implementation.

In developing an ontology of physics, or any subject, it is important to consider what is unnecessary or impractical as well as what is needed or desirable. Consider that a significant effort of research in physics today is oriented towards developing a big theory of everything (BigTOE) which would unify what are separately described branches of physical theory. One could say that this should result in the ultimate ontological description of physics. Being a subject of research, though, a BigTOE is far from being settled, and, consequently, far from being a subject that can be put forth as a standard. Even though there has been considerable success towards unifying theories in physics, a practical ontology is perhaps better based upon a less unified view, e.g., a collection of sub-domains of physics, such as kinematics, dynamics, electrodynamics, heat flow, acoustics, chemical dynamics, etc. Clearly, since fundamental physical theory is still a matter of research, it would be impractical to formulate a comprehensive ontology that captured such incompletely developed concepts as unification.

What we should aim for in a standard is an ontology that is useful for the common uses rather than an academic ideal, however correct that may be. This suggests the question, "To what degree is it feasible to standardize a description framework, or ontology, for model dynamics?" The formulation of standards should be possible whenever there is no essential disagreement on what is being discussed or described. It should also be possible to form a standard when different descriptions of a domain of knowledge have clear equivalences, such as is the case with physical units mentioned earlier.

Artificial Intelligence (AI) research into Qualitative Physics [17] has focused on various formal approaches to developing ontologies of physics. These ontologies have often, though not always, taken a formal, axiomatic structure, exploiting the inherent mathematical nature of physical theory, or concentrate on a "common sense" view of physics. They often focus in depth on a narrow class of physical problems. Formal methods approaches can lend themselves to the application of automated theorem provers which can create extensions to the ontology beyond the basic axioms. The intention of some of these ontologies might be to answer diagnostic questions such as "Why did the nuclear power plant's cooling system overheat?", or analytical questions such as "How much fuel would be required for the rocket to reach stable orbit?" Such questions reflect a desire to have computers reason deductively, as human physicists might, about physics. While it is desirable to support extensive chains of deductive reasoning that could answer such questions, it is difficult, as with any axiomatic, mathematical theory, to demonstrate that these axiomatic descriptions are self-consistent. While attempting to automate these kinds of complex reasoning is laudable, such work is still a subject of AI research. Also, while it is possible that an extended effort of development may produce these types of capabilities, it might be more fruitful to scale down the requirements we demand of an ontology so as to realize near-term results.

4.3 A Practical Ontology of Physics

The DoD M&S community currently has a collection of numerical models that possesses a fair degree of syntactic interoperability, thanks largely to the HLA. This means that the format for data passed between dynamical models has a standardized syntax. The meaning of that data is more open to question. The process of inserting a dynamical model into an HLA simulation framework provides little assurance that the insertion will create a meaningful outcome. As they are, DoD M&S dynamical models often lack a higher-level, abstract description of the analytical model of which they comprise a numerical implementation. Even if models currently possess some abstract description, there being no standard framework for which to phrase it, the scope of utility of such a description is limited to the human technical experts who can find and understand it.

As we have discussed above, there are many important questions that might be asked that we could develop an ontology to help us answer, but perhaps we should first attempt to answer simple questions. Some of the questions that we might attempt to answer first could be: "When this federate is plugged into the simulation network, will it automatically discover those models with which it may, or must, interact?"; or, "Will the model be able to communicate to other federates the services that it can provide?"; or even "If I try to couple two models together that are incompatible, will I be alerted to a reason for the incompatibility?" While these questions appear to relate to the M&S architecture, they can only be answered using the semantic descriptions of the contents of the models.

Answering such questions would be useful and does not necessarily require a great depth of reasoning. Perhaps starting with a broad, descriptive ontology would be most helpful in classifying those object dynamics that are appropriate to a given situation. As requirements dictate more definition, this can be added and the ontology refined. One idea may be to focus on a process of elimination in making a determination that a given dynamic model may be appropriate for a specific object, and not expecting a single, deterministic answer. We might make better progress by first determining the dynamic models that are almost certainly inappropriate for the object, and thereby eliminating them from further consideration, before trying to determine which of two feasible models makes better sense. Surely, it is easier to determine that a rigid-body dynamics model cannot predict the future state of the atmosphere than it is to determine which of two meteorological models is the better one to use. In any case, the determination of which is the better model is often a question that is still a matter for human debate, and so forming a standard that determines such a decision is not helpful. As time progresses and human debate settles such open questions, future standards could certainly be amended to incorporate the additional discriminants for enabling more fine-tuned decisions of appropriateness. In order to support these kinds of reasoning it would be helpful to have an abstract classification scheme within which to describe dynamical models. In the end, we envision an ontological structure that first captures fundamental physics, then details governing equations of various branches of physics such as fluid mechanics, electrodynamics, etc. At more detailed levels, standard approximations would be characterized, such as viscous fluid flow and inviscid fluid flow, and, following that, named numerical models. Additionally, we envision describing the concepts of measurement and uncertainty and the process of state estimation.

We propose that the subject of our effort should be to represent a vocabulary to express the physical concepts that may be used to describe the mathematical statements that comprise physics-based models. We include dynamical models as well as data: a language that includes, colloquially speaking, verbs as well as nouns is much more expressive than one that only includes nouns. To maintain a clear focus, however, we propose to restrict an ontology to the mathematical objects and formalisms that are actually used by applied physicists, as opposed to the concepts laymen might use. The intent is to enable these physicists to describe their models to each other and to avoid the problems and ambiguities involved with representing "common sense" descriptions. We intend an ontology of physics to capture the concepts of physical theories in a formal language so as to support various forms of automated information processing that are not currently supported. The current primary use of computers for physicists is as calculation devices, to estimate predicted values of observables. A secondary use, not formally coupled to the primary use, is for supporting documentation and communication of collected data and models. We intend for an ontology of physics to connect together in a more formal way the conceptual physics, its mathematical expression, and the consequent numerical evaluation procedures, all to better support documentation and communication.

4.4   The Semantic Web and Related Tools

We interject at this point to say that there are a variety of ontology-related tools available to help us in our objective to develop an ontology. Note that our definition of the term ontology does not specify or recommend a particular computer language mechanism to be used. At some point we will need to choose some specifics of this kind, i.e., languages and tools. Since we will need to use these tools in developing a standard ontology of physics we mention them now so as to keep them in mind as we proceed.

In the last few years the development of the Standardized General Markup Language (SGML), Extensible Markup Language, (XML) and Web Ontology Language (OWL), has led to realization of a capability to capture the ideas embodied in an ontology and put them to use in elucidating semantics within documents and data. These constructs and an associated set of ontologies and knowledge bases are being developed to create the Semantic Web. The Semantic Web is an idea conceived by the World Wide Web Consortium. Notable among these is Tim Berners-Lee, inventor of Hyper-Text Markup Language (HTML) and the first web browser, and currently director of the W3C. Whereas HTML allowed the creation and easy access and display of text-like documents, the Semantic Web consists of a set of constructs that support the representation of layers of semantic descriptors, or metadata. These metadata promise to lessen ambiguity and even support intelligent automated processing of documents on the web.

A variety of tools have arisen due to efforts of the W3C. In 2004, the W3C released the Resource Description Framework (RDF) and OWL as W3C recommendations[18]. RDF is used to represent information and to exchange knowledge in the Web. OWL is used to publish and share ontologies, supporting advanced Web search, software agents and knowledge management. Another tool, RDF Schema describes how to use RDF to build RDF vocabularies. RDF Schema defines a basic vocabulary and conventions for use by Semantic Web applications.

The DARPA Agent Markup Language and Ontology Inference Layer (DAML+OIL) [19], still another tool, is a semantic markup language for Web resources. It builds on earlier W3C standards such as RDF and RDF Schema, and extends these languages with richer modeling primitives. DAML+OIL provides modeling primitives commonly found in frame-based languages. DAML+OIL (March 2001) extends DAML+OIL (December 2000) with values from XML Schema data types. DAML+OIL was built from the original DAML ontology language DAML-ONT (October 2000) in an effort to combine many of the language components of OIL. The language has clean and well-defined semantics. OIL is a proposal for a web-based representation and inference layer for ontologies, which combines the widely used modeling primitives from frame-based languages with the formal semantics and reasoning services provided by description logics. It is compatible with RDF Schema (RDFS), and includes a precise semantics for describing term meanings (and thus also for describing implied information). A DAML+OIL knowledge base is a collection of RDF triples. These triples represent a subject-predicate-object triple, where the predicate is a relationship between the subject and the object. DAML+OIL prescribes a specific meaning for triples that use the DAML+OIL vocabulary. This document informally specifies which collections of RDF triples constitute the DAML+OIL vocabulary and the prescribed meaning of such triples.

Finally, other tools developed under the coordination of the W3C are the Mathematics Markup Language (MathML) and its extension, OpenMath. A key element of a complete framework for describing physics-based models is the language for describing mathematical concepts. We expect MathML and its extension, OpenMath, to provide the ontology. MathML 2.0, a W3C recommendation was released on 21 Feb 2001 [20]. MathML is a low-level specification for describing mathematics as a basis for machine-to-machine communication. It provides an interchange format between computer algebra systems, such as Mathematica™, Maple™, Scientific Workplace™, and MathCAD™. The impact of the W3C on the development of this technical concept representation language is clear, since MathML arose due to efforts of the W3C Math working group. The Math Activity of the W3C has been re-launched as the Math Interest Group and has a charter to continue the task of facilitating the use of mathematics on the Web, both for science and technology and education. The effort to build a standardized ontology of physics, whether or not it becomes an independent activity, will need to coordinate with the Math Interest Group for overlapping areas of activity.

4.5 The Physics-Based Model Modeling Process

To determine where to begin developing a standard ontology, we first synopsize the process a model developer uses in developing a simulation model of physical dynamics. One may visualize these steps as layers of abstraction, with higher levels of abstraction lying above lower levels. Each subsequent layer provides a representation of the layer above it (Figure 8-3).

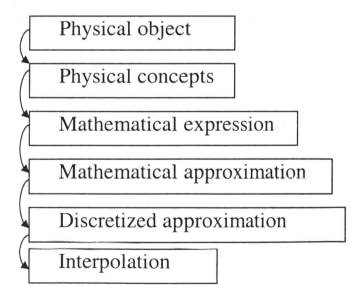

Figure 8-3. Physics-based model ontology "layer-cake".

The first decision in the modeling process is to decide what object to model, i.e., the actual physical object that is to be represented. The representation of real-world physical objects in an ontology is as a vocabulary of these objects, such as ships, tanks, missiles, the ocean, or the atmosphere. We expect that there is also a related classification taxonomy, since the human-constructed objects, at least, have many classes relating to properties that are not strictly physical, such as their purposes.

The next step a developer must take is to determine what the relevant physical concepts are that are required to model the physical objects being considered. We can call this the physical concepts layer. The physical concepts layer is used to represent the physical attributes of the physical object. We believe that of these layers, that which is least developed from the perspective of a formal description is the physical concepts layer. This layer includes the ideas of conservation, the notion of physical objects whose properties are conserved, and the properties of interactions between these physical objects.

The mathematical expression layer represents the formalized statements of the physical concepts, i.e., the laws of physics in symbolic mathematical form. This step begins with one or more fundamental physical equations, usually differential in nature. In the mathematical expression layer, the physical concepts are represented with precise statements that can be used to provide, for example, predictions of the values of future states of the physical object. From a physicist's point of view, when the physical concepts have been laid out and the mathematical expression of those concepts written down, the model is complete save for a solution. Note that the model is considered physically incomplete or incorrect if the solutions are not functional, i.e., they must have a single-valued solution for predicted values of observable properties of physical objects as functions of space and time.

Since many mathematical expressions resulting from physical models may be difficult to solve, for example, due to inefficient or poorly developed mathematical methods for finding solutions, mathematical approximations are commonly made. These approximations are often made by neglecting terms of a mathematical expression that are considered to have a small effect on the solutions. These approximations have consequences with respect to the physical concepts tied to the neglected terms. These approximations and the physical interpretation of the consequences are a common source of "hidden assumptions" in physics-based models, making their characterization particularly important. This layer may be considered part of the mathematical representation layer, or an independent, mathematical approximation layer.

Most of the solutions mentioned so far will have been expressed in continuous, rather than discrete, state spaces. They are typically expressed in algebraic mathematical symbols. For example, many of the fundamental equations of physics are differential in nature, and the final combined solution of an object's physical state, as a function of time, is typically an integral over continuous space and prior time of the influences of those things physically affecting the object.

Next, there is the discretized approximation layer. Subsequent to making mathematical approximations, lack of analytical solutions often forces us to resort to numerical, or discrete, approximation methods, in order to get an estimate of the answers we seek. Space and time are usually discretized. In the representation of the mathematical terms on the discretized space/time grid, differential equations are represented as finite difference equations and continuous integrals as discrete sums. There are multiple ways a single mathematical formulation may be discretized, which in a continuum limit are equivalent. The application of these methods to providing solutions to mathematical expressions is often ad-hoc with only weak formal justification for their use. In this process there are frequently many choices to be made, some arbitrary, some motivated by analytical reasoning, and some motivated by practicality. It is common that there is only vague comprehension of the accuracy of these methods. Sometimes models may be run at "higher resolution", or closer to the continuum limit, to improve accuracy, when it is feasible. Improved accuracy is generally gained at the expense of computational resources, where cost is often expressed in the amount of time required to arrive at a solution. Additionally, for a given discretization of space and time there may be multiple algorithmic choices. For example, to compute the area under a curve, $F(x)$, we can compute the integral by adding up the areas of a "bar-chart" representation of $F(x)$ or by applying the Trapezoidal Rule, both using the same discrete values of $x(i)$ and $F(x(i))$. The result is that different discretized solutions of the same underlying analytical equations may be considered non-equivalent. The nature of the discretization layer in the modeling process explains the common experience that there are as many solutions as there are developers. It is also a process that can make the computer code difficult, if not impossible, to relate back to the original mathematical description. The best approach to standardizing a description of the discretization of the algorithm would probably be a standard for a symbolic representation of the discrete sums and finite difference equations. A description of an algorithm using this kind of standard might well resemble standard source code itself, e.g., C++ code.

We note here for purposes of contrast and comparison that the SEDRIS standard's data representation model, or DRM, provides a means for describing discretized data fields, where the values between grid points are supplied by user defined interpolation. SEDRIS does not discuss or prescribe discretization methods, nor does it represent the underlying mathematically continuous ideal: SEDRIS is a standard for representing things that have been discretized. Certainly the standard was developed with cognizance of the variety of typical numerical methods used by computational model implementers, and so supports them without describing them. Since we would expect a standard descriptive framework of object dynamics to complement the SEDRIS standard, we here raise the interesting question as to whether it would be desirable or feasible to design an ontology of physical dynamics that referred only to discretized models.

Finally, we have the interpolation layer. The solution to the mathematical expression often entails a single, modeler-selected discretization, or grid. This approach cannot anticipate the data requirements of all possible users. For many users to have access to model output, an interpolation is often required, to determine the values on the user specified (discretized) domain, or grid, instead of the modeler-selected grid. We can call this layer the interpolation, or translation layer. Ideally, the user specifies the grid that the model computes the results for and this interpolation is unnecessary, but practically speaking, interpolation is sufficiently common that we need to represent it. This final layer, the interpolation layer, is the business end of the model, which provides the answers needed by other models.

We note two important properties of this hierarchy of conceptual modeling layers. First, there is generally a one-to-many relationship between each layer and the one below it. While there are often formal and consistent relationships that hold within each of the above described layers, transitions between layers are often not formal or consistent. Each physical object may be modeled in multiple ways. There may be variations in the mathematical statement of a set of physical concepts. There are many approximations that may be made for a given mathematical representation, and so on. As a consequence, it is difficult to infer the layer above from the layer below.

The second, related property is that, as a rule, intrinsic meaning is lost, in a sense, as one proceeds from the physical layer downwards. Additionally, precision may also be lost. What is gained is a quantifiable result - a timely, computable, numerical answer. For example, mathematical expressions may be formally combined and solved without ambiguity or lack of meaning within mathematical formalism. It is difficult, however, to infer what physical principles are being represented in the equations. Without proceeding to a discretized representation, a mathematical expression may be unsolvable with current analytic techniques. As one proceeds to obtaining a numerical answer, precision in the result may be sacrificed due to the approximations that are often made in the downward transitions.

The hierarchical layer-cake description illustrates the nature of metadata needed. For example, the physical object layer provides a context for the physical concepts that are used to model it. If we merely were to state the physical concepts and neglect to indicate what we are in fact modeling, the reader of our model is left to guess what our meaning is. While it is true that an educated reader of the model can often guess correctly what the intent of the model's author was, why leave the reader guessing? This is not acceptable in print documents, nor should it be acceptable in model representations.

The way that the Ontology Layer-cake illustration helps to understand how metadata may be utilized is that information from each layer may be used to "tag" the information from the layer immediately beneath it. This is because each layer gives the context and describes the thing that is being represented in the lower layer. For a given model, the relationships between the layers exposes the assumptions made in constructing the model.

As an alternative to the above-described multilayered modeling process, one may decide that one should use exclusively discrete models, since these are what are implemented on computers, in order to preserve formal meaning within a discrete mathematical representation. The problem with this approach is that the implemented model is far removed from the semantically-rich physics layer. As well, most physical models are specified in symbolic mathematical form and not for the convenience of programmers of discrete models. The real answer to this problem is continued research to create more formal transitions between these layers. In the meantime, we need to work within the established set of methods for these transitions, accepting the resultant, often unpredictable, errors incurred by doing so.

At this point we point out that there are some practical tools that may help in the modeling process we describe above. Many are familiar with the MATLAB™ product line, which provides an integrated development environment with the core constructs of discrete arrays and an interpreted scripting language. Other tools, such as the computer algebra systems, are based upon representing, manipulating, and solving formal, symbolic mathematical expressions. Additionally, these tools support the numerical evaluation of the mathematical expressions. Another effort, the development of the Modelica™ language, bears examination for supporting interchange of models created with computer aided design, or CAD, systems. Some of these tools may be candidates for building an ontology of physics. While one should be careful in relying upon proprietary tools for standards development so that the standards do not rely upon the specific tools, these tools do provide a current capability to express many of the concepts we have discussed. It may be that wider use of these kinds of tools alone will facilitate meaningful interoperability and should be encouraged.

While standards may be helpful in specifying each of these layers, we are focusing particularly on the physical semantics and their symbolic mathematical representations. If we believe that we can standardize the commonly accepted laws of physics, we need to determine which variation should be standardized. Because the laws of physics are mathematical, we can derive alternative equivalent formulations by algebraic manipulation. We certainly don't want to standardize each distinct permutation in the phrasing of the equations. Perhaps there is one approach to formulating the laws of physics that is better than others. For example, while most of the fundamental equations of physics are differential in nature, relating infinitesimal changes of physical state with respect to space and time, the representation of a solution to the equations is generally integral in form. Since we seek to represent a way of describing the solutions, perhaps that is the place to start.

4.6   Approach to Standardization

We note that communities of appropriate technical expertise, not the W3C, must define vocabulary semantics. This means that physicists must make the substantial contribution to our effort . However, since the W3C coordinates the formation of web standards relevant to the development of an ontology of physics, in order to have broad impact, coordination with the W3C is desirable if not necessary. The W3C can act as a coordinating mechanism for bringing together the various communities of interest for a given topic. This coordination may be effected by having status as an advisory committee representative to the W3C in order to submit proposals for new activities, such as working groups and interest groups [21]. Currently, the DoD has the Defense Information Systems Agency, or DISA, and the U.S. Navy as member organizations, and therefore having advisory committee representatives for each organization.

While coordination through the W3C may help stimulate interest in the development of discipline-specific ontologies, there are already organizations that have indicated an interest in the development of a markup language specific to physics-based documents. In particular, organizations representing large professional memberships and that produce physics publications would be interested in document metadata. Among them are the American Physical Society, the American Astronomical Society, the American Institute of Physics [22], and the International Union of Pure and Applied Physics [23]. We have begun communications with these organizations. We note, though, that the primary expressed interests of these organizations at present are to create electronic document repositories.

Nevertheless, a standardized representation of physical concepts is the common ground they share with the M&S community.

5.   SUMMARY

We have described how the development of a standardized ontology of physics should proceed, reviewing the structure of comprehensive model descriptions, the tools and organizational mechanisms available to implement the ontology, and existing standards that affect its development. We have received interest in the effort from the M&S community as well as the Physical Science membership and publications community. We expect to proceed with efforts to engage with the W3C in order to effectively build a standard for comprehensively describing physical modeling concepts.

6.   ACKNOWLEDGEMENTS

The Defense Modeling and Simulation Office has directly supported and the Navy Warfare Development Command has indirectly supported the work described in this chapter.

7.   REFERENCES

1. D. Whitney, R. A. Reynolds, D. Sherer, M. Driscoll, S. Olson, P. Dailey, "TAOS: Developing High-fidelity, Consistent Environmental Data Products for STOW 97 and UE-98-1," *Simulation Interoperability Workshop*, Paper 97F-SIW-150, September 1997.
2. C. Scannell, J. Collins, "Providing an Improved Real-Time Natural Environment for the Navy's Fleet Battle Experiments", *Simulation Interoperability Workshop*, Paper 03F-SIW-089, September 2003.
3. R. A. Reynolds, H. Iskenderian, S. Ouzts, "The Ocean, Atmosphere and Space Environmental Services (OASES) System," *Simulation Interoperability Workshop*, Paper 01S-SIW-047, March 2001.
4. J. B. Collins, T. Foreman, and D. Speicher, "A New Design for a Sonar Environmental Effects Server", *Simulation Interoperability Workshop*, paper 02F-SIW-114, September 2002.
5. T. Foreman, D. Speicher Expanded Sonar Environmental Acoustic Effects Server Capabilities for Fleet Battle Experiments,," *Simulation Interoperability Workshop*, paper 03F-SIW-062, September 2003.
6. R.M. Hodur, J.D. Doyle: "The Coupled Ocean/Atmosphere Mesoscale Model Prediction System (COAMPS), Coastal Ocean Prediction," *Coastal and Estuarine Studies* 56, pp. 125-155.

7. D.N. Fox, W.J. Teague, C.N. Barron, M.R. Carnes, C.M. Lee: "The Modular Ocean Data Assimilation System (MODAS)," *J. Atmos. Oceanic Technol*. 2002, pp. 240-52.

8. WAMDI Group: "The WAM model – a third generation ocean wave prediction model," *J. Phys. Ocean*, vol. 18, 1988, pp 1775-1810.

9. R. Allard, J. Christiansen, T. Taxon, S. Williams, D. Wakeham: "The Distributed Integrated Ocean Prediction System (DIOPS)," 7th *International Workshop on Wave Hindcasting and Forecasting*, 2002.

10. Paul W. Maassel, Richard Schaffer, Sean Cullen, Gerry Stueve, Chris Scannell, Joseph Collins, Nicholas Kim "Improving the Water Column Representation", Proceedings of the 8th Simulation Interoperability Standards Organization (SISO) *Simulation Interoperability Workshop*, 00F-SIW-060, Orlando Florida, September, 2000.

11. J. B. Collins and D. Clark, "Towards an Ontology of Physics", *Proceedings of the European Simulation Interoperability Workshop*, paper 04E-SIW-044, July 2004.

12. J. B. Collins, "Standardizing an Ontology of Physics", *Simulation Interoperability Workshop*, paper 04F-SIW-114, September 2004.

13. P. G. Foley, F. Mamaghani, P. A. Birkel, "The Synthetic Data Representation and Interchange Specification (SEDRIS) Development Project", (1998)

14. A. Tolk, J.A. Muguira, "The Levels of Conceptual Interoperability Model", *Proceedings of the Fall 2003 Simulation Interoperability Workshop*, Orlando FL, Sept 14-19 2003, Paper 03F-SIW-007.

15. International Standard ISO 31, Quantities and Units, (1992), and International Standard ISO 17, Metrology and Measurement; Physical Phenomena.

16. N. F. Noy and D. L. McGuinness, "Ontology Development 101: A Guide to Creating Your First Ontology", Stanford Knowledge Systems Laboratory Technical Report KSL-01-05 and Stanford Medical Informatics Technical Report SMI-2001-0880, March 2001.

17. B. Faltings and P. Struss, *Recent Advances in Qualitative Physics*, The MIT Press (1992)

18. Deborah L. McGuinness and Frank van Harmelen, editors. 10 Feb 2004. OWL Web Ontology Language Overview. Retrieved from W3C site: http://www.w3.org/TR/owl-features/

19. Dan Connolly, Frank van Harmelen, Ian Horrocks, Deborah L. McGuinness, Peter F. Patel-Schneider, and Lynn Andrea Stein. 18 Dec 2001. DAML+OIL (March 2001) Reference Description. Retrieved from W3C site: http://www.w3.org/TR/daml+oil-reference

20. Max Froumentin. 13 Sep 2004. W3C Math Home. Retrieved from W3C site: http://www.w3.org/Math

21. Ian Jacobs, editor. 05 Feb 2004. W3C Process Document. Retrieved from http://www.w3.org/2004/02/Process-20040205/activities.html

22. 11 Nov 2002. General SGML/XML Applications. Retrieved from the XML Cover Pages site: http://xml.coverpages.org/gen-apps.html#physics

23. Arthur Smith. 06 Nov 2001. Long Term Archiving of Digital Documents in Physics. Retrieved from American Physical Society site: http://publish.aps.org/IUPAP/ltaddp_report.html.

INDEX